The Petrie Museum of Egyptian Archaeology

CHARACTERS AND COLLECTIONS

Edited by Alice Stevenson

The Petrie Museum of Egyptian Archaeology

CHARACTERS AND COLLECTIONS

UCLPRESS

Contents

First published in 2015
by UCL Press
University College London
Gower Street
London WC1E 6BT

Text © Alice Stevenson
and contributors, 2015
Images © 2015 University
College London

A CIP catalogue record for
this book is available
from The British Library

ISBN: 978-1-910634-04-2

DOI: 10.14324/111.
9781910634042

Designed by Bobby Birchall,
Bobby&Co
Printed in the UK by
Belmont Press.

Front cover image: Painted
and gilt cartonnage mask of
the Roman period (UC45926).
Back cover image: Steatite
statuette of seated scribe,
Late 18th Dynasty (UC14820)
©Heini Schneebeli.

Page 2: A whimsical 3100-
year-old image on a
potsherd (UC15946).

Preface

There are an infinite number of ways to know a collection and no one person can ever exhaust all of the possibilities. The first aim of this book is, therefore, to bring together only a very small series of vantage points chosen by several individuals in order to introduce the range and scope of University College London's Petrie Museum of Egyptian Archaeology. Together, we can but scratch the surface of the array of objects held here and much more remains to be explored. And anyone is welcome to do so. The entire collection is available to view online (http://petriecat.museums.ucl.ac.uk/) and each object is identified with a unique number, prefaced with the letters 'UC' (which stand for University College), as are the objects in this publication.

The second aim of this book is to introduce just a few of the characters whose lives became caught up in the discovery, care and rediscovery of the collection. These are stories not just of famous archaeologists, but also of the unsung multitudes upon whose labour this Museum is built. It is therefore to the Egyptian workforce and all the staff and volunteers of the Petrie Museum (past and present) that this small volume is dedicated.

Acknowledgements

The production of this book has been a team effort. In addition to all the contributors, thanks are due to the following for their help in putting together this volume on such a tight schedule: Giancarlo Amati, Jaimee Biggins, Bobby Birchall, Iain Birkett, Andreas Effland, Ute Effland, Mona Hess, Robert Hill, Mary Hinkley, Charlotte Horlyck, Ali Hosseininaveh, Adina Iaczko, Carolyn Jones, Baoping Li, Emma Libonati, Nelson Multari, Sherry Neyhus, Paul O'Sullivan, Ahmed M. Mekawy Ouda, Ivor Pridden, Maria Ragan, Margaret Serpico, Lara Speicher, Yuanyuan Tan, Andrew Trowbridge, Roman Wisniewsk and Yijie Zhuang.

Contributors

Editor Alice Stevenson, Curator, UCL Petrie Museum of Egyptian Archaeology

Sherif Abouelhadid, Research Assistant, London School of Hygiene & Tropical Medicine.

Richard Bussmann, Senior Lecturer in Egyptian Archaeology/Egyptology, UCL Institute of Archaeology,

Debbie Challis, UCL Public Programmer, UCL Petrie Museum of Egyptian Archaeology

Kandace Chimbiri, Children's Black History author and publisher, Golden Destiny Ltd

Edmund Connolly, Museum Co-ordinator, UCL Petrie Museum of Egyptian Archaeology

Jennifer Cromwell, Postdoctoral Researcher, Department of Cross-Cultural and Regional Studies, University of Copenhagen

Pia Edqvist, Curatorial Assistant, UCL Petrie Museum of Egyptian Archaeology

Lucia Gahlin, Chair, Friends of the Petrie Museum

Tracey Golding, Visitor Services Manager, UCL Petrie Museum of Egyptian Archaeology

John J. Johnston, UCL Institute of Archaeology

Janet Johnstone, Friends of the Petrie Museum

Lidija McKnight, Research Associate, KNH Centre for Biomedical Egyptology, University of Manchester

Norah Moloney, Honorary Senior Lecturer, UCL Institute of Archaeology

Carolyn Perry, Director, MBI Al Jaber Foundation

Jan Picton, Friends of the Petrie Museum, Teaching Fellow UCL Institute of Archaeology

Helen Pike, Public Programmer, UCL Petrie Museum of Egyptian Archaeology

Campbell Price, Curator of Egypt and the Sudan, Manchester Museum, University of Manchester

Stephen Quirke, Edwards Professor of Egyptian Archaeology and Philology, UCL Institute of Archaeology.

Al-Saddiq Al-Raddi, Poet

Carole Reeves, Senior Lecturer in Science and Technology Studies, UCL Department of Science and Technology Studies

Daniela Rosenow, Honorary Research Fellow, UCL Institute of Archaeology

Amara Thornton, British Academy Postdoctoral Research Fellow, UCL Institute of Archaeology

Map of Ancient Egypt and Sudan

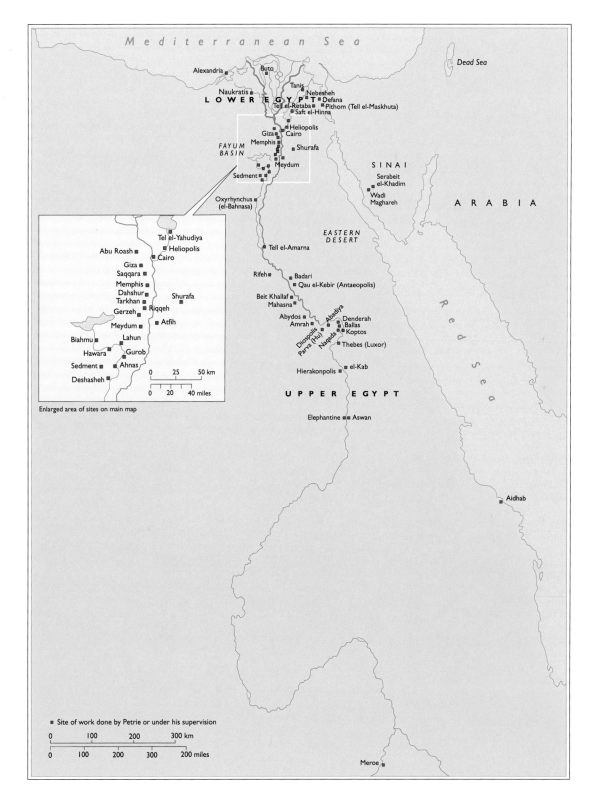

Mediterranean Sea

Dead Sea

Alexandria

Buto

Tanis

Naukratis

Nebesheh

Defana

LOWER EGYPT

Pithom (Tell el-Maskhuta)

Tell el-Retaba

Saft el-Hinna

Heliopolis

Giza

Cairo

Memphis

Shurafa

FAYUM BASIN

Meydum

SINAI

Sedment

Serabeit el-Khadim

Wadi Maghareh

Oxyrhynchus (el-Bahnasa)

ARABIA

EASTERN DESERT

Tell el-Amarna

Rifeh

Badari

Qau el-Kebir (Antaeopolis)

Beit Khallaf

Mahasna

Abydos

Amrah

Abadiya

Denderah

Ballas

Koptos

Diospolis Parva (Hu)

Naqada

Thebes (Luxor)

Hierakonpolis

el-Kab

Red Sea

UPPER EGYPT

Elephantine

Aswan

Aidhab

Meroe

Enlarged area inset

Tel el-Yahudiya

Abu Roash

Heliopolis

Cairo

Giza

Saqqara

Memphis

Dahshur

Shurafa

Tarkhan

Gerzeh

Riqqeh

Meydum

Atfih

Biahmu

Lahun

Hawara

Gurob

Sedment

Ahnas

Deshasheh

0   25   50 km

0   20   40 miles

Enlarged area of sites on main map

■ Site of work done by Petrie or under his supervision

0   100   200   300 km

0   100   200   300   200 miles

Introduction: a modest little museum

Museums are much more than the sum of what is displayed in their galleries. They are spaces in which time and space are compressed, where complex and multi-layered histories are reassembled, lost, rediscovered and contested. This occurs not only through the mix and match of objects, but via the flow of people who become caught up in the lives of objects and collections. The Petrie Museum of Egyptian Archaeology at University College London (UCL) is no exception. Despite its name, the Museum is a product of many more individuals than its famous founder, William Matthew Flinders Petrie (1853–1942), while the spatial and temporal parameters of its collection are far broader than the simple term 'Egyptian Archaeology' might popularly suggest.

There are more than 80,000 artefacts in the Petrie Museum. These have been amassed over the last 150 years through the happenstance of archaeological discovery, the opportunism of purchase, and the fortuity of gifts and exchanges. The collection ranges from implements made hundreds of thousands of years ago to a twentieth-century tapestry woven at the Wissa Wassef Centre in Saqqara, and from tiny pieces of mosaics less than 0.05 mm thick to near-life-sized stone statues of lions. The objects in the Museum's care come not only from Egypt's Nile Valley and northern Nile Delta, but also from the Egyptian deserts and from elsewhere on the African continent and the wider Mediterranean and Asian worlds. To do justice to this material eclecticism, if that is even possible, would take a publication far larger than this. Instead, our aim in this small volume is to trace out some of the contours of this assemblage and relate just a few of the unusual stories and personalities behind the technical labels and the Egyptological references.

Opposite: Map of Ancient Egypt and Sudan, showing the key sites represented in the Petrie Museum.

Below: *Dahshur Lake*, a tapestry made by Sayed Mahmoud at the Ramses Wissa Wassef Art Centre, Saqqara, Egypt (UC80605).

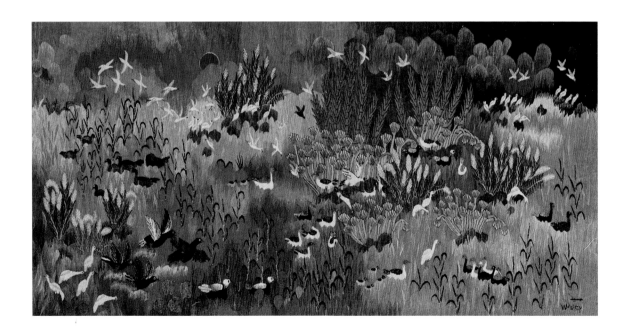

The Amelia Edwards Museum?

Today the Petrie Museum of Egyptian Archaeology is most readily associated with the personality of Flinders Petrie, who transformed the practice of archaeology and made countless discoveries in both Egypt and Palestine. In recognition of these achievements Petrie was bestowed with numerous accolades; not that he cared much for high praise. Take his pocket diary entry for 25 July 1923, for instance, which states simply: '10.30 Buckingham Palace. Knighted. Back by 12.' Such a perfunctory writing style was characteristic of the man who once said that 'I would rather do a week's hard work, than assist in a day's pleasure.'[1] It is

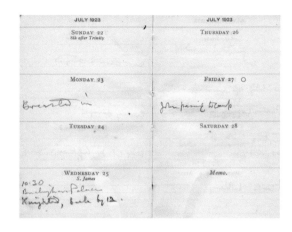

testament to several decades of such an extraordinary work ethic that the Egyptian collection at UCL is so rich, diverse and textured with histories. Yet the Museum owes its existence to a much larger cast of characters who worked tirelessly with the objects now housed here, including Petrie's wife – the archaeologist Hilda Petrie – his students, work-crews and successors. Indeed, the Museum would not be here at all were it not for the bequest of a charismatic Victorian novelist and artist who 'made Egyptology a household word'.[2]

Amelia Edwards (1831–92) was a resolute explorer, but her purpose in travelling to Cairo in the winter

Above: Entry from Flinders Petrie's pocket diary on the day he was knighted. Petrie Museum archives.

Left: Flinders Petrie in the field at Abydos in 1899.

of 1873–74 had simply been on a whim, 'for a month's sunshine, warmth, and dry weather'.[3] Her excursion, however, proved to be a turning point in her life and she returned to England a dedicated campaigner for the preservation of Egypt's heritage, devoting the remainder of her life to this cause. Edwards was instrumental in the foundation of the Egypt Exploration Fund (which continues today as the Egypt Exploration Society) and her inspirational oratory ensured that it attracted loyal supporters and admirers both in the United Kingdom and abroad. Her passion for Egypt also extended to her personal collection:

> … dearer to me than all the rest of my curios are my Egyptian antiquities; and of these, strange to say, though none of them are in sight, I have enough to stock a modest little museum. Stowed away in all kinds of nooks and corners, in upstairs cupboards, in boxes, drawers, and cases innumerable, behind books, and invading the sanctity of glass closets and wardrobes, are hundreds, nay, thousands, of those fascinating objects in bronze and glazed ware, in carved wood and ivory, in glass, and pottery, and sculptured stone, which are the delight of archaeologists and collectors.[4]

On her death in 1892 it was this ensemble of things that formed the foundation of UCL's Egyptian collection. Edwards had chosen UCL as the home for her beloved antiquities because it was the only university in England which, at that time, awarded degrees to women on an equal basis to men. This bequest was also accompanied by an endowment that established the UK's first Chair in Egyptian Archaeology and Philology. Edwards worded her bequest very carefully to exclude anyone working at the British Museum and, by stipulating that the post-holder be under forty years of age, she ensured that Flinders Petrie was the only possible candidate.

Petrie had also been amassing his own collection since 1881, by purchasing antiquities from dealers in Egypt, as well as by acquiring pieces from the excavations

Opposite top: Egyptian workmen excavating the tomb of king Den at Abydos around 1900.

Opposite: The UCL Egyptian displays of beads, photographed in 1915 (PMAN6044). The UCL Egyptian displays of pottery, photographed in 1915 (PMAN6045).

Left: Late Period (664–343 BC) figure of the goddess Bast from the Amelia Edwards collection (UC45378).

he directed for the Egypt Exploration Fund, for his private sponsors Jesse Haworth and Martyn Kennard, or through the British School of Archaeology in Egypt that he founded in 1905. For all these excavations he was dependent upon teams of Egyptian workmen, many of whom he had trained to dig carefully and who became some of the world's first excavation specialists. The teams included men such as Ali Suefi from the village of al-Lahun, who Petrie described as 'his best lad' and who was responsible for the discovery of many of the artefacts now on display in UCL. The Egyptian excavators became known as 'Quftis', after the village that many originated from. Their descendants continue to work on archaeological sites to this day.

By 1910 these collecting activities had resulted in 'a hoard which lay in layers piled on sheets of paper one over the other in the few cases at the College. Stores of larger objects had to lie in ever increasing soot and dirt.' It was, Petrie lamented, 'getting beyond my control'.[5] At this point UCL agreed to formally acquire and take responsibility for the collection, and in June 1915 what had once been hidden away by Amelia and precariously stacked up by Flinders went on display for the first time.

The Egyptian Museum, University College

An account of the new Museum was published in 1915 and it paints a vivid picture of the layout of the original displays. The new cases occupied the upper level of a whole wing of the main University building, just south of the great dome, and had a floor area that was around 120 by 50 ft (36.5 by 15 m) wide. Despite the space there

was still a clutter and jostle of objects: 'the series of pottery' alone, it was reported, 'runs nearly the whole length of the room'. Stretched across this corner of UCL was the full span of Egyptian history, neatly lined up through sequences of beads, palettes, stone vessels, scarabs, flints, figurines, weights and measures, funerary figurines and wooden tools.

The Museum was explicitly not at this time intended to attract and interest general visitors; it was for study and teaching purposes. As Petrie himself was away for the better part of the academic year in Egypt, that teaching load fell to his assistant, the 'small and energetic' Margaret Murray (1863–1963), who was later famed for being a 'white witch' on account of her widely published interest in witchcraft.[6] Despite all her responsibilities, Murray was instructed not to touch the artefacts in the Professor's absence. Petrie alone was to be in charge of the organization and labelling of displays. That, however, is not the same as cataloguing and to the horror of his successor (Stephen Glanville, 1900–56), in 1934 there remained thousands of artefacts packed away in cupboards and drawers without any form of identification to show where they had come from. Petrie had extolled the virtues of systematic object registration in a paper he wrote for the journal *Nature* in August 1889, but he unfortunately did not put this into practice in his own Museum. It was Glanville who began the systematic registration of the Museum's holdings. Beginning at UC001, he began by documenting one of the collection's highlights – the striking art of the Amarna period, produced in the city of the so-called 'heretic pharaoh' Akhenaten and his wife Nefertiti. It would take another seventy years to complete the numbering and cataloguing. It will take several lifetimes more to further research, enrich and correct the 80,000 object records that underpin so much of the Petrie Museum's daily work.

Above: Petrie in University College London in 1921.

Left: Limestone block with outline depiction of the head of queen Nefertiti, from Petrie's 1891 excavation season at Amarna (UC011).

In the line of fire

There had been an urgency to the campaigns led by Amelia Edwards and Flinders Petrie to ensure the survival of the ancient past in the face of modern dangers within Egypt. But in relieving Egypt's heritage from one set of threats, they soon – unknowingly – exposed it to another set of hazards in the Western world. Wars and natural disasters destroyed many relics acquired in Egypt and exported abroad. London was not immune to such perils, but it is thanks to the dedication of a few individuals that the Egyptian collection is still here after a tumultuous century in the UK's capital city.

The Museum's early-twentieth-century location beneath University College's skylights was a vulnerable one, not least because of the vagaries of the ever-unpredictable British weather, but also because it posed a significant security risk. Petrie had been especially agitated during the zeppelin raids of the First World War, but UCL escaped unscathed and the collection continued to grow in size as 'Petrie's pups' – the students he trained out in the field – took on their own excavations. Among this new generation of fieldworkers were Guy (1878–1948) and Winifred Brunton (1880–1959), as well as Gertrude Caton-Thompson (1888–1985), who all worked in the Badari region of Egypt revealing Neolithic (fifth millennium BC) material for the first time in the country. Even a young T. E. Lawrence – the famed 'Lawrence of Arabia' – joined a Petrie excavation in January 1912, describing the Professor as 'easy-tempered, full of humour, and fickle to a degree that makes him delightfully quaint'.[7]

Below: Photograph from Gertrude Caton-Thompson's album from the 1924 excavation season at Badari. Labelled from left to right: 'Mrs Aitken, Miss Don, Mr Starkey, Mr Back, Mr and Mrs Brunton'. Petrie Museum archives.

During the Second World War the UCL campus was not so lucky and it suffered a direct bomb hit that gutted the Egyptology Department. Fortunately, as the clouds of conflict gathered across Europe, hasty plans had been executed to remove the most important artefacts out of London, while the majority of what remained had been boxed up in 160 tea chests and carried to the vaults by a band of loyal students and staff, including Elise Baumgartel (1892–1975) and Violette Lafleur (1897–1965). But even here, in the depths of the University, the ancient objects were still at risk and when firemen hosed down UCL's burning central structure, waters flooded the subterranean floors and the sanctuary where the storage crates were held. With the rest of the staff called up for war duties, it was left to Lafleur to almost single-handedly conduct the continuous salvage programme that ensured the collection survived.

The Petrie collection remained in storage after the war, and heavy thunderstorms left several crates standing in water. It was not until 1949 that work started on 'temporarily' rehousing the collection in an old local department store's stable (Shoolbred & Co) situated above the Malet Place boiler house. Seventy-five years later, the Petrie Museum is still in its cramped, temporary accommodation.

Above: The burnt dome and ruins of the College building caused by the bombings of 1940 and 1941. UCL Special Collections Digital Archive.

Below: The Petrie Museum in 1953 (E.ng. 3632).

The bulk of the post-war labour associated with unpacking and redisplaying the collection became the responsibility of a new Egyptology lecturer at UCL – Anthony (Tony) Arkell (1898–1980). Management of museum collections was second nature to Arkell, who had set up the Khartoum Museum in Sudan in the 1940s. Setting up the Petrie was a mammoth task, but one that was duly acknowledged in Arkell's *Times*[8] newspaper obituary as being one of his many life's achievements: 'students of Egyptology', it noted, 'owe him a massive debt'. By 1953 a large part of the collection was set out in its new home, just in time for the celebrations of the centenary of Flinders Petrie's birth.

The trauma of war had taken its toll on the objects in the collection and in 1953 a new technician, Martin Burgess, was hired to attend to the most vulnerable pieces. He was still fairly new to the post when a fire broke out in his laboratory, igniting highly flammable chemicals and consuming the wooden floors. In the smouldering chaos Burgess sifted through the debris for some of the material he had been working on, including a large stone vessel with the image of the goddess Hathor. Several sheets of papyrus were also soaked in the firemen's rescue, but remarkably none were lost.

The quest for a new home

Threats to the Petrie collection did not abate as time marched on through the 1960s, 1970s and 1980s, with floods, leaks, fumes and vibrations causing endless problems. Despite the poor conditions the collection was still swelling in size. Fewer objects were allowed to be exported from Egypt by this time, but nevertheless, significant groups of material from fieldwork were still entering the collection. This included finds made during the UNESCO rescue campaigns in Nubia in the 1960s, when the Aswan High Dam was set to flood large swathes of both modern homes and ancient landscapes. Harry Smith, the then Edwards Professor and Petrie Museum Curator, was part of the team that excavated an enormous ancient Egyptian military fort at Buhen, some of the finds from which were transferred to the Museum. The acquisition of material from other, private, collections further added to the volume of objects in the Museum. The collection of Sir Henry Wellcome (1853–1936), the pharmaceutical magnate, arrived in 350 packing cases in 1964. Most of the material was subsequently dispersed to other museums, but a significant proportion, notably Sudanese antiquities from the royal city of Meroe, were officially registered into the collection. Then, in 1970, several hundred cat figurines were bequeathed to the collection by Mrs Langton.

With all these new additions the Museum space had become packed from floor to ceiling, but the building

Below: Protective amulet called a 'cippus' showing the god Horus as a child, standing on two crocodiles with oryx and serpents in each hand. Formerly in the Wellcome Collection (UC2341).

around it was steadily deteriorating. An appeal was launched in the early 1980s to raise funds to construct a purpose-built building. It was sadly unsuccessful and, in the aftermath, rumours of a sale of the collection circulated through the University offices. Fortunately, such a disposal never transpired. Some relief in the form of renovations led by Curator Barbara Adams (1945–2002) were initiated, and despite the constraints of space, an increasingly active public programme commenced in order to bring in school groups and larger numbers of university students. In 1988 the Friends of the Petrie Museum was founded to support conservation work on the collection, raising funds through social activities, lectures and seminars. This supported the conservation of many highlights in the collection, including the Fayum mummy portraits and a rare bead-net dress.

In 1998 the entire Petrie Museum collection was designated by the UK Government as being of national importance. Such a status opened up new sources of funding that allowed the collection to move beyond the limitations of its accommodation at least virtually, through a computerized database. Under the direction of Roy McKeown, the 1999–2002 digitization project placed the Museum among the first institutions in the world to have pictures and information on nearly every single object accessible online.

Museum futures

A change in Egyptian legislation in 1983 brought to an end the finds division system that had allowed Western collections to expand in the late nineteenth and early twentieth centuries. Only exceptionally were small numbers of 'gifts' made to foreign excavations at the discretion of the Egyptian authorities. Since the 1990s no antiquities have been allowed to leave Egypt whatsoever and the Petrie Museum no longer receives material from fieldwork, nor will it seek to purchase artefacts from the problematic antiquities market. While there is no need for the Petrie Museum to continue to acquire antiquities, this does not mean that it cannot actively collect modern material that might help to interpret, illustrate or encourage new readings of archaeological collections, for example by working with artists and communities culturally connected to the Nile Valley. Through these means, and through our outreach programme, the Museum today focuses on addressing the legacy of archaeological work and collecting practices that were conducted during the high point of British colonialism in Egypt.

This expansion of perspectives was first signalled by the award-winning travelling exhibition *Digging for Dreams*, mounted by the Petrie Museum in 2000–01 under manager Sally MacDonald's lead and curated by Dominic Montserrat (1964–2004), which sought to present new ways of looking at ancient Egypt and archaeology. The central part of the temporary show tackled complex subjects relating to the relationship between ancient Egypt and societies today, including concerns about the collection and display of human remains, issues of race and Afrocentric perspectives on Egypt, the relationship between modern and ancient Egypt, the

Opposite: Painted and gilt cartonnage mask from the Ptolemaic or Roman period (305 BC–AD 395), conserved with the support of the Friends of the Petrie Museum (UC45926).

impact of colonialism on the discipline of Egyptology and the reception of ancient Egypt in science fiction, esoteric religion and other areas. This initiative to open up the collection to new audiences has remained central to the Museum's curation, research and outreach activities ever since. Research in the Museum archives by former Curator, now the Edwards Professor of Egyptian Archaeology and Philology at UCL, Stephen Quirke, has challenged the well-worn narrative of archaeological exploration in Egypt, which is frequently presented as the outcome of heroic endeavours of individuals. Flinders Petrie is one such figure who features prominently in exhibitions and publications around the world as 'the father of Egyptian archaeology', but his work built upon the labour of 'hidden hands',[9] including Egyptians and women. Small interventions, in the form of photographs of such individuals, have been placed within the confined and crammed spaces of the old-fashioned display cases at the Museum in homage to their archaeological contribution. Other endeavours have embraced the digital age with the development of high-quality 3D computer models and reproductions of objects in the collection, together with apps such as *Tour of the Nile*, which can be downloaded free from the internet, http://www.ucl.ac.uk/museums/petrie/research/research-projects/3dpetrie/downloads/app-tour-of-nile.

Above: Flyer for a Petrie Museum event in November 2014.

The areas covered by *Digging for Dreams* have also been the blueprint for public programming and audience development. The Petrie Museum's current activities for external audiences aim to look at the ancient past and modern receptions of that past from different viewpoints, including those traditionally disregarded by academic Egyptology. Our public programme of events and outreach activities aspires to put different academic disciplines, artistic practices and ways of thinking together. Two recent examples from 2014 are *Festival of Pots* and *A Fusion of Worlds: Ancient Egypt, African Art and Identity in Modernist Britain*. *Festival*, with the support of the Petrie Museum Friends, worked with a collective of ceramic artists, Manifold, to interrogate the Museum's vast collection of pots, Petrie's ground-breaking sequence dating system and the uses of pots, as well as to create new artistic work with local audiences within Camden. In our *A Fusion of Worlds* exhibition and programme of events we collaborated with UCL Geography's Equiano Centre and members of the public to reconsider how Egypt was received by African diaspora audiences and how it was used in anti-colonial identity politics in Egypt and Jamaica during the interwar period. This brought in new audiences asking challenging questions about race and identity within Egyptology.

The Museum does not only provide a space for engagements with ancient Egypt and Sudan. It also seeks to make links with the modern countries whose heritage is in its care. In 2013, for instance, the Petrie hosted an event for the anniversary of the 25 January 2011 Egyptian revolution, with two short videos and a commentary from Egyptian PhD student Ahmed Mekawy Ouda. It was, he said, 'a moving speech'. That same year Ahmed helped to organize a presentation on 'History Rewritten: Ancient Egyptian Art revived through post-revolutionary graffiti in Cairo' by the Egyptian writer and journalist Soraya Morayef.

In the past ten years, the Petrie Museum has also acquired a reputation for hosting ground-breaking events for Lesbian Gay Bisexual and Transgender (LGBT) History Month, assisted by our partnership with Camden LGBT Forum, and for the use of contemporary academic ideas on sexuality, identity and representation in the ancient and modern worlds. We run a thriving film club exploring Egypt and the ancient world on screen, airing everything from cult TV, such as *Xena Warrior Princess*, to Hammer horror movies such as *She,* in order to understand and showcase so-called 'alternative' receptions of Egypt and antiquity. In these ways we work towards making events and programming more participatory by giving people a platform to articulate their passions and ideas about the collection.

Above: Ahmed Mekawy Ouda at the Petrie Museum in May 2013.

The Museum has not, however, forgotten its roots as a teaching and research collection. Hundreds of scholars consult the collection every year for a diverse range of scientific, historical and artistic studies, while the teaching potential of the collection now extends beyond its obvious and long-standing links with archaeological, museological and conservation programmes. We now additionally accommodate any course that is able to think laterally about the place of objects and archives in learning: chemistry, psychology, history, geography, engineering and astronomy are just a few of the subjects the Museum has worked with in the last few years. Too often is Egyptian archaeology seen as a niche and specialist area, but it has potential relevance that extends far beyond disciplinary boundaries.

Today, in the early twenty-first century, the Petrie Museum of Egyptian Archaeology, and the collection that it contains, might seem modest in size, but it is certainly not modest in the quality of its holdings, nor in the aspirations of its outreach.

Alice Stevenson *Curator, Petrie Museum* and
Debbie Challis *UCL Public Programmer, Petrie Museum*

Artefact displays in the Petrie Museum, around 2001. In many respects the displays are better understood as a form of visible storage.

Violette Lafleur: bombs, boxes and one brave lady

Only one tin of Ptolemaic funerary masks and thirty limestone tomb-wall fragments were deemed beyond repair following the bombing raids of the Second World War. It is remarkable that more was not lost. We owe this to one incredible lady who, through sheer determination, took up the challenge of packing and sorting the collection during this tumultuous time. Against a backdrop of wartime austerity and danger, Violette Lafleur managed almost single-handedly to save the Petrie collection.

In 1938 the most fragile and most important objects in the Petrie collection began to be boxed up and moved to the Blockley, Gloucestershire home of a naval Captain, George Spencer Churchill, a cousin of Winston Churchill. The bulk of the work was undertaken by Lafleur, with the occasional assistance of College porters and a former student. The remaining 160 cases stayed on campus in the South and Refectory Vaults.

On 18 September 1940 the College sustained bomb damage that destroyed the skylights, allowing water to drip onto a tray of funerary cones and wooden toys. Despite this close shave, Lafleur returned a few days later to continue her efforts at considerable personal risk: one day a bomb dropped nearby as she laboured over the collection.

Below: Photograph of Violette Lafleur in her conservation lab. Petrie Museum archives (E.neg. 3631).

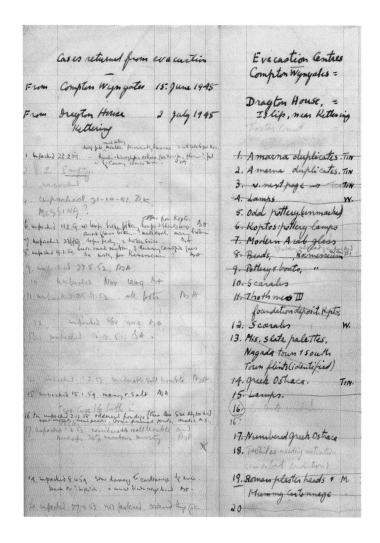

Above: Wartime packing list. Petrie Museum archives.

It was arduous work, compounded by the lack of packing crates due to wood shortages, meaning Lafleur had to improvise with drawers and trays. Then, in April 1941, the College suffered an almost direct bomb strike and, although artefacts were not directly damaged, water from the firemen's hoses seeped into the basement, leaving cases standing in water. The artefacts had to be unpacked, dried, treated and repacked once again.

Funds were eventually secured from College coffers to finish the last tranche of repacking and some 405 cases were transferred to Compton Wynyates in Warwickshire, where part of the British Museum collection was already safely housed. As the bombs continued to rain down it was clear London was far from safe. The Ministry of Works arranged for a further 275 cases to be moved to Drayton Court in Northamptonshire, home of Colonel Stopford Sackville. By July 1943 some 14 tonnes of cases and crates had been transported by the Pall Mall Depositing and Forwarding Company in four separate van loads, all sorted and designated by Lafleur.

Her valiant efforts were noted at the time and the then-Provost, David Pye, asked that an official letter of appreciation for her efforts be written. There were plans to further acknowledge her remarkable achievements with a plaque. This never materialized, and only a short speech was given at a UCL Fellows dinner in May 1951.

Lafleur had no formal academic qualifications and her professional status at UCL was something of an anomaly. With her extensive experience of collections care and management, she was eventually bestowed the title 'honorary museum assistant', a role that she held until her retirement in 1953. She never received a single penny for her work, nor was it ever commemorated in the way that she deserved. Her commitment, however, is not forgotten.

Helen Pike

The earliest evidence for people in Egypt: the first tools

Stone tools indicate that humans had lived in Egypt for 400,000 years before the pyramids of the Old Kingdom were built. Until about 6,000 years ago these people led a nomadic lifestyle, moving from one place to another during the year in search of food. These were groups of hunters, fishers and plant collectors who did not build permanent homes or settlements but lived mainly in the open landscape. As neither pottery nor metal tools had been invented, they made tools from stone and other organic materials such as wood. Wooden tools are rarely preserved, but many thousands of stone tools have been found which reveal much about human life in the Palaeolithic.

In Egypt, people usually made stone tools from chert, a siliceous rock with properties that allow the stone-worker to control the way it breaks. Chert occurs both as pebbles and in rock outcrops. It is often possible to identify the exact outcrop that was the source of specific tools, and this can show how far from their campsites early groups went to collect suitable stone. Chert is broken by striking it with a pebble called a hammerstone; good hand–eye coordination is needed to strike the chert in the right place and with the right amount of force so that it fractures as the tool-maker wants. Broken chert fragments (flakes) have razor-sharp edges and can be used immediately, but they can also be further chipped and shaped for tasks other than cutting. It is possible to re-sharpen a dull edge or re-shape a tool, and when the tool is no longer useful it is thrown away. Archaeologists specializing in stone tools can often determine all or part of these stages in a tool's life history: the source of the stone, how and where the tool was made and shaped, how and on what it was used (for example, for butchering meat or working wood), and where it was discarded. Such information gives us a glimpse of how groups of humans lived so long ago.

The Petrie Museum has thousands of stone tools spanning the Palaeolithic to New Kingdom periods. Some tools, such as Predynastic

period daggers, required great skill and were made by specialists, but most people would have known how to make tools for daily use.

During the Middle Palaeolithic (roughly 350,000 to 70,000 years ago) a method of manufacture known as Levallois was common. The skilled tool-maker carefully prepared the chert block (called a core) to remove a flake of a pre-determined shape. Scars on flake and core surfaces indicate flakes removed during preparation and shaping stages. Levallois tools may look easy to make, but modern experimental replication shows that the technique is extremely difficult to achieve without hours of practice.

Many Palaeolithic tools from Abydos now in the Petrie Museum, including the flakes and core pictured, were collected by Gertrude Caton-Thompson in the 1920s and 1930s. She first went to Egypt with Flinders Petrie in 1921, later returned to direct her own excavations, and subsequently had a distinguished career in archaeology.

Norah Moloney

Out of this world: prehistoric space beads

On 28 June 1911 a small farming village near Alexandria witnessed a fearful column of smoke as a meteorite fell to Earth with a sound like an explosive clap of thunder. It was the first meteorite ever reported in the country, but this was certainly not the earliest Egyptian encounter with space debris. Five thousand years previously another small Egyptian community may have been equally awestruck by rocks descending from the sky. Even if Egypt's prehistoric human inhabitants did not see the event, when the remains were found the unusual nature of this iron-rich meteorite must have caused quite a stir. It was not like any substance then known, as the Iron Age was still 2,000 years away. Despite the novelty of the material, the Egyptians were still able to work the brittle metal carefully into delicate beads. These were then strung with other exotic stones and finally laid to rest in a grave dug in the earth, near the modern village of el-Gerzeh, around 3400 BC.

Today those extra-terrestrial fragments are in the Petrie Museum in the form of three corroded brown-grey lumps. They are the world's oldest known examples of worked iron. They may not look much now, but experimental archaeology by Diane Johnson of the Open University has demonstrated just how striking the appearance of heated meteoric iron can be, with its metallic sheen and vibrant fluorescent colours. That these beads were regarded by prehistoric Egyptians as something special is evident from the other valuable things found in the grave numbered '67'

Above: Predynastic bead made from meteoric iron (UC10738).

Below left: Original excavator's drawing of Grave 67, Gerzeh.

Below: Original excavator's notes on the contents of Grave 67, Gerzeh.

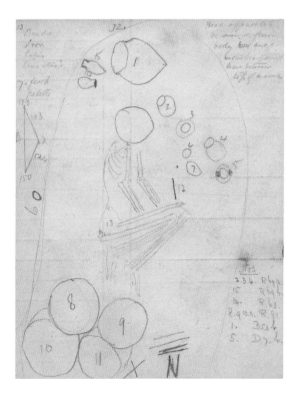

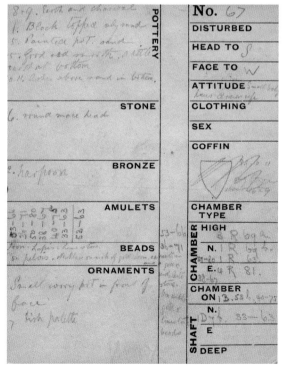

by the excavators. We are fortunate that the excavation records of the cemetery of Gerzeh, where the beads were found, survive today in the Petrie Museum archive, along with some of the other artefacts found. The tomb assemblage included beads made of bright-blue lapis lazuli, a stone whose closest source to Egypt was in Afghanistan, as well as gold and carnelian from Egypt's Eastern Desert. The grave offerings also included a hippopotamus ivory vase, a copper harpoon, a limestone mace head and a fish-shaped palette, used for grinding the vivid green copper ore malachite into a pigment. It was a unique and eclectic group of things.

Fieldwork at Gerzeh was completed in 1911, the same year that the Egyptian meteorite made the headlines in Egypt and internationally. The excavation director, Gerald Wainwright, must have been aware of the stories circulating in the press and scientific networks. His own theories of the meteoric origins of the ornaments were thus timely, but it would be another century before his identification was fully confirmed through analytical chemistry. In 2013 a team led by Thilo Rehren of UCL examined the chemical composition of the beads, proving that the combination of elements was consistent with extra-terrestrial rocks.[10] Neutron imaging revealed the internal structure of the beads, which were hammered to be only 1 mm thick, then rolled, not drilled. Given the coarse and inelastic nature of the material, this demonstrates just how skilled prehistoric Egyptian smiths were.

Alice Stevenson

Abu Bagousheh: Father of Pots

Flinders Petrie was good with numbers. He liked nothing better than to measure, calculate and plan. These were the skills that allowed him to create the world's first detailed prehistoric timeline using nothing but pottery, paper and a pencil.

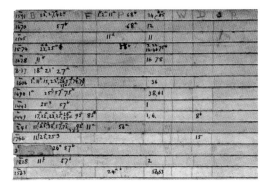

In 1894–95 Petrie's teams unearthed thousands of striking pottery vessels from a large necropolis at Naqada. At first Petrie thought that the discoveries were 'wholly un-Egyptian',[11] but when it was realized that these were in fact prehistoric – Predynastic period – ceramics, he set about trying to create order from the mass of finds. He had always argued that pottery was important for archaeologists and his workmen had given him the nickname Abu Bagousheh ('Father of Pots') because of this.

Using codes for each different pottery type, Petrie listed the contents of individual graves on thin strips of card and began to sort them. He noticed things like different types of decorated pottery that were never found together in the same tomb, and he separated these graves into two groups. By continuing to group together pottery types, grouping like with like and separating out dissimilar forms, Petrie arranged

900 slips into an order. He called it 'Sequence Dating'. Petrie's method is now known to archaeologists as a type of seriation, a complex statistical procedure for which we usually require computers today. Petrie had managed to do it all on paper via a sort of nineteenth-century spreadsheet. Mathematicians are also impressed by his achievement; it was the first instance of mathematical modelling in archaeology.

Pottery is as crucial for dating the historic periods as it is the prehistoric, and Petrie's teams recovered vast amounts of it: almost 10 per cent of the Petrie collection is ceramic material. Not all of the pottery was made along the Nile. Many of the vessels in the collection are imports from surrounding countries, including Syria, Palestine, Cyprus, Crete and Greece. By the Islamic period the range of imports even included ceramics from China.

Alice Stevenson

Right: Display of pottery in the Petrie Museum, including a stone bottle with the names of Rameses II and Queen Nefertari written in blue-filled hieroglyphs (UC16427).

Lost and found: the rediscovery of the Tarkhan dress

1912 was an intense season of excavation for Petrie. As he led his team systematically surveying, recording, excavating and mapping a group of mastaba tombs at Tarkhan, an Early Dynastic cemetery 59.5 km south of Cairo, he entered Mastaba 2050 to find that the contents had been sacked in antiquity. Nevertheless, using his years of experience, Petrie located a quantity of linen cloth under the sand alongside some white stone jars, a lid from a pot and wooden handles for tools. In general, linen was discarded as worthless by the majority of archaeologists at that time, but Petrie preserved all good evidence of materials and artefacts that could throw light on the daily life of the ancient Egyptians.

The rescued bundle of linen from Mastaba 2050 was packed away with other finds and sent back to UCL for further analysis, where it lay untouched for sixty-five years. Rosalind Janssen (neé Hall), the Assistant Curator at the Petrie Museum and textile expert, rediscovered the Tarkhan linen in 1977 and fully appreciated its importance.[12] A conservation plan was put in place and from the filthy, muddy bundle, Sheila Landi, the textile conservator at the Victoria & Albert Textile Conservation Workshop, unearthed a small, long-sleeved dress with pleated sleeves and bodice, in remarkable condition. The dress has a V-neck and is simply made from three pieces of sturdy hand-woven linen with a natural pale grey stripe, which complements the neatly knife-pleated sleeves and bodice. The hem is missing so we do not know if the dress was short or long, but its dimensions would indicate that it fitted a young teenager or a slim woman.

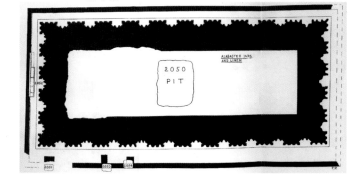

The date of the dress is contentious. Although Carbon-14 dating in the 1970s was breaking new ground, it required the destruction of a large piece of dress fabric. The decision was made not to test the textile, but to use relative dating from associated artefacts from the Tarkhan site. The dress was dated to Dynasty 1 (3100–2890 BC), making it the world's earliest example of a constructed garment.[13] Later testing by the British Museum Research Laboratory confirmed that the finds from the Dynasty 1 Tarkhan mastabas were probably later in date than the burials, and therefore the dress, by association, was assumed to be Dynasty 5 (2494–2345 BC). Until the dress can be safely tested we are still unsure.

Sheila Landi recalls working on the little dress. As she removed the caked mud, she revealed the creases in the sleeves at the elbow and under the arms created by the owner who had originally worn it. Suddenly, Sheila felt that ancient life speak once more from nearly 5,000 years ago, reverberating through a simple linen dress that was lost and found again.

Janet Johnstone

Above: Flinders Petrie's drawing of Mastaba 2050, inside which the linen dress was found.

Opposite: Linen dress, at least 4,500 years old (UC28614B1).

The lost lions of Koptos

How do you lose two near-life-sized stone lion statues? That was the question that puzzled Petrie Museum Curator Barbara Adams in 1980 after she had spent a year cataloguing the Museum's collection of rare, early Egyptian material from Petrie's 1893–94 excavations at Koptos. Adams knew that Petrie had noted in his diary for January 1894 that 'we have also found two large lions in limestone … we can put back these animal figures to the prehistoric time as they cannot be of any known age of Egyptian art'.[14] Late nineteenth-century records showed that fragments of these beasts had been sent to the UK, but they had since disappeared.

When Barbara finally found them it became obvious why they had been overlooked for eighty-six years. The lions were not in a few large chunks: they were in pieces that numbered in their many thousands. The mass of chipped limestone had been stuffed into six wooden tea crates, along with a few larger pieces, at the Wellcome Institute for the History of Medicine. Henry Wellcome (1853–1936), the pharmaceutical magnate, had sponsored Petrie's British School of Archaeology in Egypt and in return Petrie sent to him a range of material in 1927, including what remained of these monumental cats.

Reconstructing the lions out of this debris was the daunting task that conservator Richard Jaeschke tackled in the 1980s. It took many painstaking months of work with the giant jigsaw before the lions' features were successfully resurrected.

Reassembled, the seated lions measure just over 1.3 m in length and are almost 0.75 m in height. In form, their closest parallels are delicate ivory statuettes found around the burials of Egypt's first kings around 3000 BC. Partly on this basis, the

Left: Small ivory lioness gaming piece from a grave at Abydos, dating to around 3000 BC (UC15506).

Koptos lions are estimated to be about 5,000 years old, making them among the earliest life-size animal statues in the world. What they once meant or symbolized is not clear. As a pair, it is tempting to envision them side by side, acting as fearsome guardians to an ancient temple. That, however, is only one of many possible interpretations. Whatever they once meant, for the time being they guard the inner sanctum of a modern-day institution: the office of UCL's Provost.

Alice Stevenson

Right: Former Petrie Museum Curator, Barbara Adams, with one of the reconstructed Koptos lions.

King Catfish and his mud seals

Little is known about Egypt's first king, Narmer. He is considered by some scholars to be the first king of Dynasty 1 and he is often credited with uniting Upper and Lower Egypt into one kingdom. Others place him in the period just before Dynasty 1. Whatever the political reality, his name was undoubtedly widely known at the time; it has been found on objects such as jars, potsherds and tablets in locations ranging from Syria in the north to Nubia in the south.

Among these records are a group of mud seals, excavated by Petrie's teams in 1912 at Tarkhan. Several seals were found between the pottery vessels of Tomb 414. Being made of mud – a mixture of clay and sand, with impurities such as chopped straw, seeds and grit – they are very fragile. The conditions for preservation of organic materials were exceptionally good at Tarkhan, and as a result these mud seals, along with other objects made of wood and linen, have survived.

The seals are imprinted with the name of king Narmer, several variations of which exist. One version is made up of the symbols of a catfish (*Nar*) and a chisel (*mer*). These early royal names are set within

Above: Drawing of the name of Narmer.

Left: Mud seal with the name of king Narmer (UC16077).

Above: Set of lapis lazuli beads found in an Egyptian grave of 3400 BC (UC5432). Since lapis is only found in Afghanistan it is evidence of networks of exchange stretching across the Near East.

Right: Limestone cylinder seal, possibly from Mesopotamia, found in an Egyptian grave of 3400 BC (UC5374).

a frame called a *serekh*, a rectangle with the falcon god Horus represented above. The *serekh* might be a representation of the royal palace, and with Horus sitting above it the reading seems to be that Narmer's royal power was divinely ordained.

The mud seals were used as 'lids' for pottery jars. The mouth of the jar would have been completely sealed by mud, placed onto the vessel opening when wet, smoothed over to the mouth edge, and sun dried. These particular seals also have traces of black pigment on the surface, which might mean that they were painted, maybe to highlight the markings.

The impression was probably made using a cylinder seal rolled across the mud surface while it was still wet, a technique that was developed in Mesopotamia (the area that now includes Iraq, north east Syria and part of south east Turkey). The Petrie Museum houses one of the earliest known cylinder seals from Egypt – a small, brown limestone piece carved with an abstract design that might represent a fish swimming in water. Dating to around 3400 BC, it was found in a grave at Naqada by Petrie's workmen in 1894–95. It might not be original to Egypt, however. This small artefact may have travelled hundreds, if not thousands, of kilometres from where it was originally made somewhere in Mesopotamia 5,500 years ago. It raises intriguing questions about the influence of the Near East on Egyptian society.

Pia Edqvist

Pulling early kingship together

In 1898, shortly before Flinders Petrie discovered the tombs of the first pharaohs at Abydos, James Quibell (1867–1935) and Frederick Green (1869–1949) were working at the site of Hierakonpolis, south of modern Luxor. They found the spectacular palette of Narmer (see *King Catfish*, p. 40). The palette is the earliest monumental representation of a pharaoh and, for many today, it embodies the origins of Egyptian civilization. Yet the more the Narmer palette was vested with symbolic value by Egyptologists, the further it was dissociated from its archaeological context.

The palette was found in a temple deposit, together with more than 2,000 votive objects, including the two illustrated here. The Petrie Museum is blessed with a range of artefacts from this trove, from royal valuables to fairly simple items. This large fragment of a mace head, with its formal depiction of a king seated on a throne opposite a dancing courtier, is similar in dimensions to the Narmer palette. In contrast, the crude limestone baboon holding its baby is more playful and intimate. Like the mud figurines and natural stone pebbles found in the same deposit, it might have been offered by people without access to the materials and technologies of kings and courtiers. Seeing the royal palettes and mace heads from Hierakonpolis in the context of local votive practices, and given the almost complete absence of royal objects in other early Egyptian shrines, one starts to wonder whether early kingship was more of a local affair – much less grand than its portrayals on the palettes and mace heads suggest.

The 1960s and 1970s bestowed a second life on the objects from Hierakonpolis. While an American team recommenced fieldwork in the temple area, Barbara Adams, co-director of the mission to Hierakonpolis and later Curator of the Petrie Museum, laid the foundation for a fresh interpretation of the material. Merging information from Green's unpublished pocket

Above: and Opposite: Two fragments of a ceremonial mace head or mace heads, found at Hierakonpolis in what the excavators called 'The Main Deposit' (UC14898 and UC14898A).

Left: Limestone statuette of a baboon and its baby (UC15000).

diaries, the excavation reports and object labels, she was able to define groups of associated objects and identify their location at the site.

Adams' research in archives and collections brought to light a wealth of objects excluded from the original reports. Adams documented all objects from Hierakonpolis kept in the Petrie Museum. Her books *Ancient Hierakonpolis* and *Ancient Hierakonpolis: Supplement* are among the first in Egyptology to make ample use of archival material and to develop publication of the Petrie collection through a site-based rather than a typological approach. It remains the only comprehensive documentation of material from Hierakonpolis in any one collection. Today, the temple and town area of Hierakonpolis are gradually vanishing from the ground. Objects and archives are all that will be left from a once-flourishing settlement that is considered to be a birthplace of pharaonic civilization.

Richard Bussmann

Above: Normal sized example of a mace head (7 cm tall) from Hierakonpolis (UC14944). These weapons were attached to a handle and many were possibly just a symbol of status.

A face in the crowd: chance encounters with Egyptian sculpture

The Petrie Museum is rightly famed for the number of objects that have come from documented archaeological excavations. However, not everything in the collection was acquired through fieldwork. Flinders Petrie also prided himself on having a good eye for antiquities and he often took advantage of the Egyptian market to fill in gaps in his artefact sequences. Sometimes he was simply lucky and, as he noted in 1915, 'good things have turned up in the most unexpected manner'.[15] This is certainly true of a rare sculpture that he acquired in Cairo some time during the early 1900s.

One evening after dinner, Petrie found himself besieged by a lively crowd of antiquities dealers, each cajoling the well-known archaeologist to purchase their curios. In the chaos a stone head rolled out of a bag and on to the floor. When Petrie looked down he found himself staring at 'the finest piece of 1st dynasty sculpture that is known'.[16] For Petrie this limestone head was a representation of none other than Narmer, considered by many to be the first king to rule all of Egypt (see King Catfish, p.40). If that identification is correct, it is the earliest known royal sculpture from Egypt.

A century later, Petrie's original theory has been challenged. Nonetheless, the style of this unusual figure is rare and intriguing. More recently, Egyptologists have scrutinized the anonymous king's features – the widely spaced eyes and protruding ears – and recognized in them the face of Khufu, the famous Old Kingdom king who was the owner of the Great Pyramid at Giza. Despite Khufu's association with one of the seven wonders of the ancient world, his image is only securely known from a small and fragmentary ivory statuette now in the Cairo Museum, which was found during Petrie's excavations at Abydos. Could this Petrie Museum object be the face behind the Great Pyramid? Or is it one of his sons, king Menkaure? Whoever it is, for Petrie such objects gave a direct insight into the ability of a society to produce sculpture and he considered this face to be a product of one of the best periods of Egyptian art. These were entirely subjective judgements, however, as the Museum's 2014 *Fusion of Worlds* exhibition, focusing on Modernist art in Britain, highlighted. The Narmer head has clear parallels with Modernist work by artists such as Jacob Epstein and Ronald Moody, yet Petrie publicly denounced the 'primitive barbarism' of Epstein's work in the 27 July 1929 edition of the *Manchester Guardian*. While Petrie might not have appreciated their work, Epstein and Moody were enchanted by Egyptian forms. Indeed, for the Jamaican-born Moody, it was 'the irresistible movement in stillness'[17] of Egyptian art in the British Museum that first inspired him to become a sculptor.

Alice Stevenson

Above: Stone vessel bought by Petrie with the name of king Khufu, owner of the Great Pyramid, written in hieroglyphs, c. 2600 BC (UC15817).

Left: Small, 5,000-year-old Prehistoric figurine excavated at Qau, chosen by the public as the lead object for the *A Fusion of Worlds* exhibition (UC9601). Photograph by Anna-Marie Kellen, Metropolitan Museum of Art.

Opposite: Limestone head of a king bought by Petrie, who thought it depicted king Narmer, c.3100 BC (UC15989).

Best foot forward: items of ancient Egyptian dress

The fashion designer Yves Saint Laurent is famously quoted as saying 'Fashions fade, style is eternal' and this is one fitting way to think about the diverse array of items of clothing and footwear in the Petrie Museum. It is particularly true for one of the rarest items in the collection: a 4,500-year-old bead-net dress currently on display amidst a gallery of pottery, one of only two such dresses known in the world.

No one knows precisely when the dress was last worn and yet it looks so 'now' and ever so 'couture'. The aesthetic qualities of the dress transcend different fashion eras, from the 1920s Flapper dress to the fishnet trend of the early 1980s. This striking garment would not look out of place on an international catwalk even today. Comments such as 'it's incredibly contemporary' are frequently heard from visitors.

Like many items of high fashion, the bead-net dress was probably quite uncomfortable to wear, given the weight of the many thousands of beads from which it is made. It also would have been rather noisy, as each of the 127 shells around the fringe are plugged with a small stone: these would have made a rattling sound when the wearer moved. For this reason it has been suggested that it might have belonged to a dancer, and it probably would have been worn over a linen undergarment. The dress was excavated in the 1920s from a

Below: Pair of Roman woollen socks (UC16766).

Bottom: Remains of a red leather slipper, possibly of Byzantine date, excavated at Hawara (UC28279i).

Right: Bead-net dress excavated from a grave at Qau (UC17743).

robbed tomb at Qau; fortunately the box that held the faience beads and shells that made up the dress had survived the robbery.

Of course, no outfit would be complete without footwear, of which there are many examples in the collection. This includes late Roman period woven socks, like those opposite, that could be worn with sandals in cooler months, and white leather boots UC28277i. Object UC28279i, shown opposite is a beautiful embroidered single red slipper with a decorative gold-coloured edging. The loose fragment shows a single motif: ornamental or symbolic? Such an item could easily be construed as the inspiration for the personalization of belongings that some of us still favour today. With the tale of Cinderella echoing in our minds, we may ask: who wore it? What happened to the other slipper?

UC16353 is a pair of miniature model clay boots, part of a number of items found by Flinders Petrie in an early Roman period child's burial at Mazghuneh. Traces remain of the red sole, which is reminiscent of a distinctive feature of shoes designed by Christian Louboutin, a French shoe-make popular in well-heeled couture circles.

Tracey Golding

Pyramids in the Petrie

At the London Hippodrome in June 1930 a special performance was staged, showcasing Egyptian history and the research of Flinders Petrie. Act III was the 'Pyramid Age' featuring the 'power and vision' of the builder of the Great Pyramid, Khufu (p. 44). That iconic monument was billed then, as it so often is today, as 'the wonder of the ages … all modern theories as to the significance of this pyramid are in vain'. Flinders Petrie himself was first drawn to Egypt in 1881 in order to measure this massive structure and to test theories about its meaning. How was it built? What was it for? Two objects in the Petrie Museum provide some small insights.

Although the mass of stone in the Great Pyramid is astounding, what is less well known is that during the reign of Khufu's father, around 2613–2589 BC, far more stone blocks were carved, moved and assembled, because Sneferu had not one pyramid built, but three. His first pyramid at Meydum was a stepped structure, but his second, at Dahshur, was to be the first true pyramid with sloping sides. It was, however, started at too steep an angle and engineers had to change their plans rapidly. The result was the Bent Pyramid. A third pyramid nearby was more successful, but nevertheless Sneferu sent his workers back to Meydum to transform the stepped structure into a true pyramid. It was this process of trial and error that provided the experience that Khufu's teams needed in order to build his colossal tomb at Giza. And it is these logistical matters that we catch a glimpse of in the Petrie Museum, in the form of a rough block of limestone with accounts, in black ink, written by workers recording the numbers of blocks of stone transported to the Meydum building site. Other blocks in the collection from the pyramid itself record dates of delivery (for example UC14482). These are testament not to commanding kings, but to the ordinary individuals (not slaves) who erected these wonders.

These records are some of the only written texts from early pyramids. The Great Pyramid at Giza does not have any decoration inside it, only the marks left by those that built it. A few centuries later, when pyramids were smaller, the royal burial chambers began to be covered with sacred hieroglyphic texts. These are the Pyramid Texts, the earliest extensive religious writings in Egypt, and they give further clues as to one of the purposes of a pyramid. Such texts were formulae that ensured the eternal existence of the king in the Afterlife. The Petrie Museum cares for an inscribed piece from king Pepy I's burial chamber (2321–2287 BC); the chamber had been destroyed in antiquity. The five columns of text on the Petrie fragment were recitations that allowed the spirit of the king to ascend and sustained him with food and drink for eternity.

Alice Stevenson

Above: A piece of stone waste used by ancient Egyptian workmen to tally up the number of blocks of stone delivered for building the pyramid at Meydum (UC30877).

Opposite: A fragment of Pepy I's Pyramid Texts (UC14540).

UC14318

An offending member

Unlike many museums with significant collections of Egyptian material, the Petrie has a limited number of monumental pieces. Nevertheless, there are a few sizable examples. One of the largest was, for about a century, also a big problem.

In 1893 Petrie directed excavations at an important ancient Egyptian religious site called Koptos in southern Egypt. Temple after temple had been erected there in ancient times, although only parts of the Ptolemaic-Roman (c. 300 BC–AD 395) sanctuary were still standing in Petrie's day. Below and around these, however, Petrie's teams found the remains of earlier buildings and statues, including portions of a Middle Kingdom temple wall dating to around 1956–1910 BC. These were carved exquisitely in relief. Some sections of these walls were shipped back to Britain and sent to places such as UCL.

One of the finest stone carvings found shows a king, Senusret I, engaged in a ceremonial run before Min, the god of fertility (below). As a deity of procreation, Min stands tall with his erect phallus directly facing the king. Such an assertive pose was an affront to the sensibilities of Victorian and Edwardian society. In other instances where

Below: Image of a limestone block with the image of king Senusret I during a ceremonial run before the god Min (UC14786).

Min was depicted, Petrie had published drawings in such a way as to omit the offending part, but this particular scene was so fine that it deserved to be photographed. Delicate censorship was therefore called for. To solve the dilemma, Petrie had his assistant, Margaret Murray, write out a large, rectangular cardboard label which was duly pasted over Min's protruding member.

The museological 'fig-leaf' covered Min's distinguishing feature for decades. Even until relatively recently there existed nervousness around exhibiting such an explicit scene. In the 1980s Cambridge University declined to take both portions when the object was loaned for exhibition, leaving Min behind at the Petrie, while Senusret went on his run alone.

Above: Graeco-Roman period terracotta model of a procession carrying a large phallus (UC33595).

Similarly, still tucked away in storage are dozens of examples of male genitalia, mainly from the Roman period. Many of these objects show a crouching figurine with legs open displaying an enormous phallus (for example UC48360). These would probably have been used as amulets, protective symbols or emblems of fertility.

Perhaps the most interesting 'phalloi' from this period are the seven terracottas showing an enormous phallus being carried in procession. These are recorded in the Museum catalogue as coming from the city of Memphis, for centuries the capital of Egypt (UC33595–601). These are very unusual objects and may illustrate fertility rites. There is a question mark over their provenance as they were not published by Petrie in his Memphis excavation reports and the limited information about them indicates they may have been part of the Wellcome Collection, which came to the Museum in the 1960s. However, the provenance and collection details of these rare processional phalloi remain a mystery.

Debbie Challis and Alice Stevenson

Wandering wombs and wicked water:
the 'gynaecological' papyrus

Menstrual cramps, bladder infections, pregnancy testing, miscarriages, labour pain, birth injuries and the menopause all featured in the lives of women in ancient Egypt, as they do today. This is vividly apparent from one of the world's oldest medical texts, excavated between 1889 and 1890 at the Middle Kingdom town of Lahun, where pyramid workers and artisans lived over a period of about a hundred years. The ancient hieratic text was written on papyrus during the reign of king Amenemhat III (1831–1786 BC), and is today joined by a modern notation: a Petrie Museum accession number (UC32057).

The surviving content has been translated by Mark Collier and Stephen Quirke and the words give us some insight into how the ancient Egyptians conceived of a woman's body and the ailments that afflicted it. For instance, the womb symbolized femininity, but it was also believed to cause many illnesses because it was an impure excretory organ – blood, babies and placentas all tumbled out of its mysterious interior. The 'gynaecological papyrus' describes several conditions.

Examination of a woman who is ill from her womb wandering

The womb was not considered to be a static organ, but one that moved around the body, wreaking havoc. This concept, first mentioned in the Lahun papyrus, remained common in the West until the eighteenth century AD. The Greek word *hustera* (womb)

Below: Medical papyrus excavated at Lahun in 1889 (UC32057).

gave us the term 'hysteria', a form of emotional instability stereotyped as feminine and believed to be the result of erratic movements of the womb.

Examination of a woman aching in her urine
You should say of it 'it is discharges of the womb'

This is descriptive of cystitis or a bladder infection causing a burning sensation when passing urine. Cystitis is much more common in women than men because they have a shorter urethra (the tube leading from the bladder). Bladder complaints could have been related to schistosomiasis, an infectious disease common in ancient (and modern) Egypt. This disease is caused by the life cycle of water-borne snails. Their parasitic larvae penetrate human skin and develop into worms that migrate to the liver and lay their eggs in the intestine or bladder, causing pain and bleeding.

Determining a woman who will conceive from one who will not

You should place a bundle of onions 'mouth on belly'

Families in ancient Egypt may have been relatively small so fertility and safe childbirth were important. Onions and wine mixed together and placed in a woman's vagina ('mouth on belly') supposedly stopped menstruation. This does not imply that a woman was bleeding more than usual but that menstrual blood might be diverted to form and nourish a baby. Aristotle, the Greek philosopher, believed that women contributed all the material to produce the baby while males produced the child's form or shape. These ideas remained part of accepted knowledge about human generation right up to the seventeenth century AD, when the first microscopes made eggs and sperm visible.

Carole Reeves

Right: Two fragments of a Middle Kingdom ivory birth wand with images of deities associated with child-birth (UC16382)

Ali Suefi of Lahun and the gold cylinder

In the winter of 1913–14, Flinders Petrie assigned to his younger colleague Reginald Engelbach (1888–1946) the task of supervising excavations of cemeteries and houses along an outcrop of sand and rock within the Nile's floodplain, just east of al-Lahun. Delayed by the First World War and its aftermath, Engelbach published the results a decade later, under the site name *Harageh* (1923). Among the burial finds were outstanding examples of jewellery dating to around 1850 BC, including one masterpiece, somewhat drily recorded in the report:

> *Tomb 211 (Middle Kingdom). This large tomb stood by itself to the North of cemetery A and had been partially robbed … In a corner of the chamber we found a very fine cylinder amulet … The core is of copper, and the gold casing very thick. On this casing are soldered small globules of gold to form a series of inverted triangles.*[18]

This amulet is one of the earliest and finest Egyptian examples of granulation, a technique known earlier in Iraq, and presumably introduced from there to Middle Kingdom palaces. The goldsmith individually soldered 3,600 tiny gold globes to form neat rows of triangles. The ring at one end enables the cylinder to be strung as a pendant. The core case contained three copper pellets and tiny fragments of organic material, perhaps to increase the protective properties of the cylinder for its ancient wearer.

The English 'we' ('we found') in the published book conceals the identity of the actual finder; fortunately, in the Petrie Museum archives, the find index cards for fifty of the Harageh tombs, including number 211, gives the initials A.S. – Ali Suefi, or, in one fuller version, Ali Muhammad Suefi, a fisherman from al-Lahun. For over three decades, Ali Suefi was effectively not just the right hand, but both eyes, for Petrie and other English dig directors. In his youth Ali Suefi was training other Egyptian excavators for Petrie at Amarna in 1891; in 1923 he identified the earliest valley-edge sites in the Badari area, which have given their name to the 'Badarian' period of Egyptian prehistory. His name has not yet entered any archaeological Hall of Fame, but the archives and the objects in the Museum show how much more we owe to him, than to many who are, for now, better known.

Stephen Quirke

Above: Ali Suefi, photograph in the Petrie Museum archives.

Opposite: Gold cylinder amulet from Harageh Tomb 211 (UC6482).

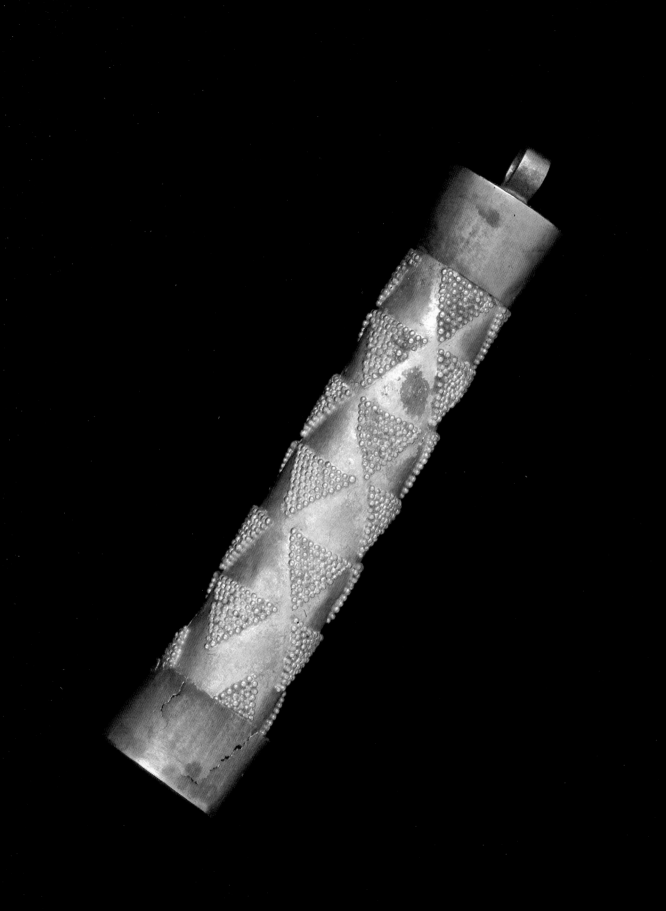

Seth: seductions and stelae

The enigmatic figure of the god Seth is one of the longest attested of the Egyptian pantheon. He appears time and again with his high, squared-off ears and his long, downturned muzzle – a recognizably outlandish appearance for a deity who is most frequently the outsider. The Petrie Museum holds a number of items that enrich our appreciation of his complex nature.

The first and, perhaps, most important, is a fragmentary and heavily damaged literary or religious text (seen opposite), probably dating from Dynasty 12. It was excavated by Petrie at the town of Lahun in April 1889, among an assortment of unrelated papyri.[19] We are told by the talented philologist Francis Llewellyn Griffith, when the text was first published, that the 'fragment relates to an episode hitherto unknown'.[20] Griffith's unease with the document is palpable. He translated it from hieratic into Latin, rather than English. The source of his disquiet is apparent: the text relates Seth's endeavour to sexually seduce his nephew, Horus, with the purpose of discrediting him and gaining the throne for himself.

Greater context for this problematic fragment was not attained until the discovery in 1928 of a more complete version of the tale. It was found amidst a library formerly owned by the New Kingdom scribe Kenherkhepeshef and it details the legal, physical and magical conflicts of Horus and Seth. However, the later text is more pragmatically brutal in its handling of the fragmentary Petrie episode, which is more concerned with Seth's flattery of Horus. Although Seth's cunning is clearly evident in the Petrie text, it is apparent in this earlier text that both deities are willing participants.[21]

It is, however, indicative of the Egyptians' complex attitude towards Seth that a New Kingdom temple was erected to him at his historic cult centre of Naqada, just north of modern Luxor. Excavated by Petrie in 1894–95, it revealed a small but important corpus of objects now held by the Museum, including a tiny, brilliantly glazed steatite stela, depicting Seth in his established part-animal form and bearing the inscription, 'Excellent praised one, beloved of Seth'. This stela appears, through its diminutive beauty, to reveal some level of personal devotion to this most multi-faceted of deities.

John J. Johnston

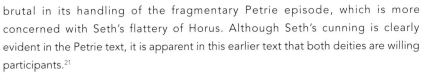

Above: Small, green-glazed plaque with the image of the god Seth (UC45093) dating to Dynasty 18 (1550–1295 BC).

Opposite: Ancient papyrus fragment, excavated in April 1889, with part of the Tale of Horus and Seth (UC32158).

Termites and tapioca: the survival of Amarna's colours

It is a wonder that painted wall decoration has survived at all at Tell el-Amarna. At this site are the remains of Akhetaten, the city founded on the eastern bank of the Nile around 1340 BC by Egypt's innovative royal couple Akhenaten and Nefertiti, who broke with tradition by worshipping only the Aten (the sun disk). Scenes adorned the walls of their palaces, painted on a layer of mud-plaster spread over mud-brick walls. Termites tunnelling through the mud-plaster and eating the straw binder have made the plaster extremely friable.

The best-known fragment of Amarna painted plaster is probably the stunning scene of Akhenaten and Nefertiti's daughters, with their rounded bellies and elongated skulls, housed in the Ashmolean Museum in Oxford. But it is less well known that the Petrie Museum is home to at least sixty fragments that may have originally formed part of this 'princesses panel' and at least ninety fragments from companion scenes on other walls in the King's House. This building was part of the pharaoh's estate, linked to the main palace by a bridge, and standing alongside a temple to Akhenaten's chosen deity, the Aten.

The colours of the painted fragments are glorious – blues, oranges, yellows. Glimpses of the royal family and their servants, hieroglyphs in cartouches, and snatches of cushions, carpets and decorative friezes give us a feel for the rich, vibrant court, and reveal a tender display of a pharaoh's family life – an intimacy not usually expressed in Egyptian royal art.

Petrie described the precarious process of moving fragments of painted plaster from ancient palaces to museums in his *Seventy Years in Archaeology*. He bemoaned the fact that the Ashmolean Museum coated the 'princesses panel' with varnish, 'sadly darkening and yellowing it' and seemingly 'destroying the most interesting dusting with powdered orpiment'.[22] Petrie's own solution to preserving the colour was a thin coating of tapioca. The fragments of plaster in the Petrie Museum retain their original, fresh colours.

The excavations he directed at Amarna in 1891–92 were the first real excavations at this large site – a daunting prospect which he compared to exploring the ruins of Brighton.[23] He felt that 'the ancient Egyptian and the modern Egyptologist had plundered [the site] as completely as they could',[24] and seemed to expect to find very little. This could not have been further from the truth, and the site continues to yield extraordinary finds to this day.

Petrie's work at Amarna was forced to an end after only six months. He wrote to his friend Francis Llewellyn Griffith, 'One year of life is enough to give to a single king and his works',[25] but in truth it was the death of his 'cordial and constant' friend and supporter, Amelia Edwards, that took Petrie back to England.

Lucia Gahlin

Above: Three pieces of plaster from the Amarna royal palace showing: (a) the face of Akhenaten (UC2267); (b) Nefertiti's name written in a cartouche (UC2261); (c) a priest (UC2277).

Opposite: Limestone relief carving of Nefertiti (UC038).

The sacred geometry of music and harmony

'If your heart is wounded, cure it with music, for music revives and elevates the soul.' Al-Tanbura (Egyptian folklore band)

The ancient Egyptian gods were concerned not only with how to preserve sacred language, but also how to create a medium through which the sounds of wisdom could travel across the empire. By adding a kinetic dimension to abstract words, ancient Egyptians created a vessel in which their stories, events, festive prayers and hymns could be contained. According to Plato's *Laws* it was only in Egypt that melodies, chants and music were uncorrupt. Contradicting the notion that ancient Egyptians were more occupied with death than life itself, they developed the science and structure of harmony, sounds and music, through which they rejoiced in their *Opet* Festival, went to war, harvested their crops and connected with the gods. Hallowed by the goddess Hathor, many musicians achieved a prestigious rank that granted them immortality.

Born and raised in timeless Cairo, I found myself embedded within a melting pot of cultures. Behind the great city's traffic lights and crowded streets lies the music of ancient wisdom. My journey across Egypt to connect the wandering soul of mine with its origins led me to the conclusion that ancient Egyptian music is still guarded by Hathor. In Upper Egypt, Sufi chanters still adopt the same posture as 'Iti, a singer depicted more than 4,000 years ago on a tomb wall at Saqqara. Clapping to adjust rhythm and tempo is inherited in a form of singing in Upper Egypt known as 'Al Kaf', which means 'palm' (it stands for clapping). Singing while feeding a child can be seen in every street in modern Egypt. Last but not least, one word used to describe the act of singing (*hst*) in the ancient Egyptian language is still used in modern Egypt to ask someone 'to describe sounds "*Hs*"'.

My journey led me to the Petrie. Touring around the displays and seeing a flute reminded me of the songs that are sung to the Nile in Egypt's Nubia today, just as the ancient Egyptians sung to the river thousands of years ago. However, what really

Left: A bronze *hes* offering vessel (UC14239) (1069–945 BC) inscribed with the name of the lady Nestanebetisheru, daughter of the High Priest of Amun, and 'great chief of the musicians of Amun-Re...'. From a burial in the royal cache at Deir el-Bahri.

Above: Faience figure of a man playing a double pipe, excavated at the Middle Kingdom town of Lahun (UC16684).

Right: Head of the Goddess Hathor (1550–1295 BC), from a vase of very thin gold, bought by Flinders Petrie at Hawara (UC28052).

captured my heart were the small statues of animals playing music. These statues portray the importance of music and also resonate with the concept of a global celebration. Finally, one artefact, hidden somewhere among the collection, managed to revive my childhood memories. This instrument, the sistrum, once played by kings or queens, is now used as a toy to make sounds by kids in modern Egypt. Musical instruments that are now displayed silent were once used to stir hearts across an incredibly wide spectrum, from soothing one's heart in prayer to igniting a soldier's heart with vengeance in war. The sound of ancient Egypt's celebration of life is still echoing. If Egypt had given the world nothing but scales, melodies and music, that alone would suffice to make it the world's greatest civilization.

Sherif Abouelhadid

Reconnecting across the centuries: fragments from Abydos

What are the chances of two teams of archaeologists, separated by more than a century, stumbling across small fragments of the same object while working across a wide expanse of desert? Quite high, as it happens.

At the turn of the nineteenth century Flinders Petrie's teams were trawling through the sands around the tombs of the first rulers of Egypt at Abydos. One of the thousands of things discovered during those excavations was a small sherd of pottery marked with the name of the Dynasty 22 pharaoh, Osorkon I (c. 922–887 BC). Today this ancient inscription is accompanied by a modern one: a Petrie Museum registration number (UC39681). This little artefact has been tucked away in storage in London for more than 100 years.

Now, in the twenty-first century, a new generation of archaeologists are working at Abydos and among the many new finds that they have made are ceramic fragments that join exactly with the sherd seen below. What makes these discoveries so remarkable is the sheer number of pottery sherds of almost all periods of Egyptian history that are strewn across the surface of this part of Abydos. It is this feature that gives the

area its modern Arabic name Umm el-Qa'ab, which means 'mother of pots'. Despite the odds, researchers such as Andreas Effland have been able to identify several more links between the pottery fragments found by the Deutsches Archäologisches Institut and those portions recovered by Petrie's workers more than a century ago.

More directly associated with the 5,000-year-old royal tombs at Abydos excavated by Petrie's workforce are other types of artefact fragments that have similarly spent decades in the drawers of the Petrie Museum, waiting to be pieced back together. These are made of a fine-grained, slate-coloured stone called greywacke. Individually, the pieces seem unimpressive, but put them together and beautifully crafted bowls in the shape of leaves emerge. Although the burials of Egypt's first rulers have been heavily plundered for millennia, such objects show how richly furnished they must have been around 3000 BC.

Alice Stevenson

Above: The Umm el-Qa'ab at Abydos. Copyright Alice Stevenson.

Left: A recently excavated sherd being compared virtually with a sherd excavated by Petrie's teams a century ago (UC39681). Copyright Ute and Andreas Effland.

Opposite: Reconstructed Dynasty 1 bowl from the Abydos royal tombs (UC35653).

'While skulls bobbed around on the waves ...': retrieving Horwedja's *shabtis*

Excavations at the site of Hawara count among Flinders Petrie's more intrepid adventures. In particular, the 1888–89 clearance of deep shaft tombs gives a glimpse of an Indiana Jones-style character at work. Tomb shafts at Hawara led to several underground chambers containing intact burials of the Late Period (664–525 BC). Unfortunately, their contents had been submerged due to the high water table in the region. (Hawara lies near the lake in the Fayum, a large fertile area some 60 km southwest of modern Cairo.) This flooding, however, did not deter the then thirty-five-year-old archaeologist.

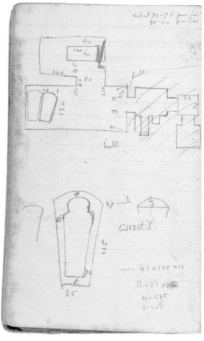

Told by workmen of the discovery of 'images as big as candles', an excited Petrie rushed to the scene. Entering the tomb was, Petrie recounted, like the 'descent into Hades' and required him to strip off his clothes in order to plunge into the foul water of one of the subterranean burial chambers. One sarcophagus was flanked by two concealed compartments, each containing a large number of funerary figurines known as *shabtis* (or *ushabtis*). Because of the brackish nature of the water, Petrie had to keep his head above the water level and try to dislodge these *shabti* figures with his feet,[26] 'while skulls bobbed around on the waves'.[27]

The *shabtis* he recovered – 399 in all – were of exceptional quality. They belonged to a man called Horwedja, a priest of the goddess Neith. The *shabtis* were made of a crushed sand/quartz substance called faience and were between 19 and 24 cm in height, ranging in colour from olive green to white due to the waterlogged conditions of the tomb. Although Petrie originally believed that they dated to Dynasty 26, the style of the figures identifies them as the work of Dynasty 30 (380–343 BC).

Petrie described the assemblage, with a glowing sense of pride, in his journal:[28]

> *Next morning, I gazed on the great stack of ushabtis in my tent, as a sort of solidified phantasy; they are about the biggest, the finest, and the greatest pile that I have ever seen of such.*

Above: Page from Petrie's notebook (39c–e) showing a plan of Horwedja's tomb.

Opposite: Three *shabti* figures from the tomb of Horwedja collected in 1888–89 (from left to right: UC28055, UC28061, UC28060).

Ever mindful of conservation, he recorded in his journal entry for the week 13–19 January 1889 that the *shabtis* had repeatedly to be soaked in water to remove the salts from them. With typical meticulousness, Petrie sorted the *shabtis* according to workmanship and speculated that seventeen moulds were used.[29] Horwedja's 399 *shabtis* are now dispersed in collections around the world, including the Petrie Museum which cares for six examples.[30] The largest single group – of fifty-eight examples – is now in the Manchester Museum, a major beneficiary of the work of Petrie's teams.

Campbell Price

Left: Portion of hieroglyphic text written for a man called Mentuhotep, governor of the district of Armant in the Middle Kingdom (2024–1700 BC). (UC14333.)

Revealing animals: discoveries inside funerary bundles

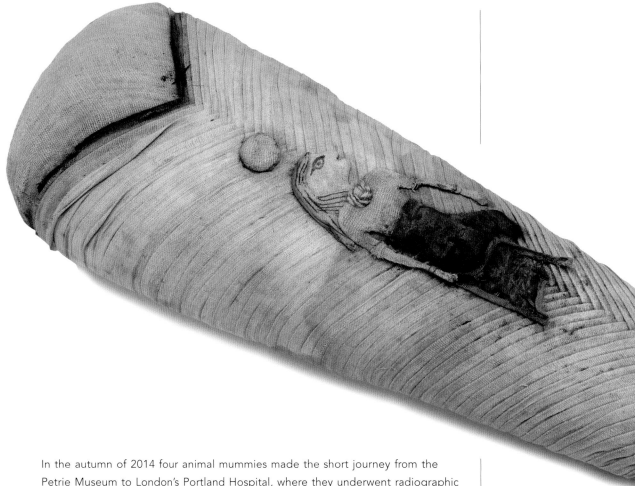

In the autumn of 2014 four animal mummies made the short journey from the Petrie Museum to London's Portland Hospital, where they underwent radiographic investigation. For the first time since their mummification over 2,000 years ago it was possible to see what was concealed beneath the wrappings. All was not quite as it at first appeared.

The research was undertaken by the KNH Centre for Biomedical Egyptology, University of Manchester, which has been investigating animal mummification since 2000, utilizing a combination of X-ray and CT scanning techniques. The ability to use non-invasive techniques without causing damage is important from the standpoint of museum ethics, where the preservation of artefacts for future generations is paramount. Since 2010, these data have been added to the Ancient Egyptian Animal Bio Bank, which is aiming to bring together data, images and scientific analysis on animal mummies in museum collections outside Egypt.

Of the four mummies studied, one was found to contain a complete and articulated skeleton of a bird (UC30709). A second mummy (UC55008), previously suspected to contain the remains of two crocodiles lying side by side, had this identification corroborated by the radiographic investigation. Two ibis (*Threskiornis*)

Above: Mummy bundle containing an ibis bird, decorated with the image of a goddess (UC30690).

Opposite: CT scan of a mummy bundle (UC30693), revealing the crushed remains of three bird eggs. Courtesy and copyright HCA International Portland Hospital.

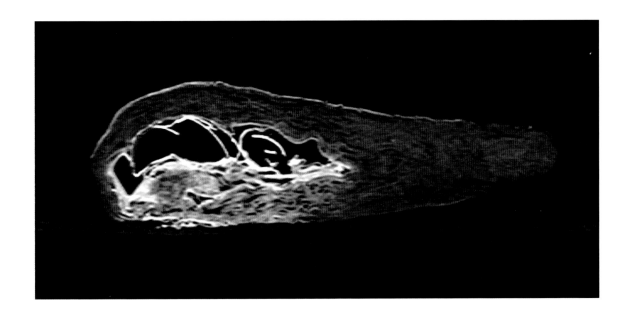

mummies, both recorded as coming from the late first millennium BC animal necropolis at Saqqara, yielded interesting results. Both mummies had been embellished by appliquéd decorative motifs on the upper surface, intended both as an aesthetic device and to identify them to the god Thoth, the god of wisdom and writing, to whom the ibis bird was held sacred. One, shown opposite, appeared to contain an ibis skeleton, although it is not clear from the fragmentary state of the remains whether the animal was complete at the time of mummification. The second ibis mummy shown above, however, was found to contain no skeletal material whatsoever. Instead, radiography showed that the widest section of the bundle enclosed the remains of three eggs, most likely belonging to the sacred ibis (*Threskiornis aethiopicus*), alongside single feathers laid longitudinally to add support to the bundle.

The mummification of non-skeletal material associated with sacred animals was not unusual in ancient Egypt. In fact, analysis of 300 wrapped bundles has demonstrated that between a quarter and a third of all animal mummy bundles contain no skeletal remains. Originally interpreted as ancient forgeries on the part of the embalmers intending to dupe potential purchasers, the current view suggests that the Egyptians chose to venerate material which had come into contact with these animals in life and was therefore considered worthy of rejuvenation in the Afterlife.

The investigation of the animal mummies of the Petrie Museum demonstrated that although the exterior of the two ibis mummies would once have looked very similar, the internal contents have proved to be very different indeed. First impressions can be misleading.

Lidija McKnight

Miw: the Langton Cat Collection

To every cat-lover – and the increase in their number is coincident with the advance of civilization – a Book of Cats is always welcome. In this book, Mr. and Mrs. Langton have shown that here, as in so many other matters, Ancient Egypt led the way and exhibited both common sense and imaginative power.[31]

Evidently a cat-lover herself, the Egyptologist and anthropologist Margaret Murray reflects on the worship and affection granted to the cat in ancient Egypt, in her review of the Langtons' book *The Cat in Ancient Egypt*. Published in 1940, the book was based on their collection of cats in various forms, shapes and guises. The Langton Cat Collection seems like a curious anomaly in the Petrie Museum. The various cat figurines – amulets, bronze sculptures, busts and jewellery – were not excavated, but acquired by Henry Neville Langton (1874–1948) and his wife from dealers to illustrate the cult of the cat in Egypt. First publishing on their collection in the *Journal of Egyptian Archaeology* in 1936, Henry Langton reflected on the symbolism of the cat, the links to other gods and their use, whether for worship or as domestic tokens of affection.

Known as *miw* in ancient Egyptian, cats are intimately associated with Egypt. The earliest representation of them is as hieroglyphs, with visual images becoming more prolific during the New Kingdom. Cats held a semi-divine status from Dynasty 22 (946–715 BC) through into the Ptolemaic and Roman periods; they were venerated for their fertility and, like the god Bes with whom they were associated, were considered to be protectors of pregnant women and young infants.[32] Today, the Langtons' feline figurines can be used to engage with cat-lovers (and -loathers), young and old, not only as a way of thinking about differences in worship and human attitudes to animals, but also because their acquisition was evidently so affectionately made. The ancient Egyptian figurines came into the Petrie in 1970, while ninety-four cat figurines from different periods produced outside of Egypt went to Norwich Castle Museum.

The Langtons' cats exemplify a serious issue in regard to the collection of antiquities. In his 1936 article, Langton refers to buying a bronze cat with a nose ring from 'a native dealer' in 1924 and admits that even at the time he doubted the antiquity of the cat, but 'of the antiquity of the nose ring there can be no doubt'.[33] The collection of specific objects for a specific purpose could lead to the acquisition of forgeries, because dealers – then as now – supply the existing demand. How many of the Langton cats are real and how many fake?

Debbie Challis

Above: Hilda Petrie with a cat, Jerusalem 1934. Petrie Museum archives.

Opposite: Late Period bronze cat from the Langton Cat Collection (UC42562).

Myth and science: ancient glass collections

Glass was a valued commodity in the ancient world. Until the mid-first century BC it was still a relatively rare material, and significant enough that there were stories told about its discovery.

One of the earliest tales comes to us from Pliny the Elder, who described in his *Natural History* (78 BC) how a Phoenician merchant ship laden with *nitrum* (= natron, a salt used in mummification) moored at the mouth of the river Belus. Located in modern Israel, the river lies near an area where glass was indeed produced in ancient times. As the merchants prepared their meal, they propped their cooking pots on some of the natron cargo. The cooking fires fused the natron to the sands of the shore, causing a translucent liquid to emerge: glass had been invented. Science tells us that this story cannot be true, however, since glass objects are known from much earlier periods, and the temperatures an ordinary campfire produces are far too low to make glass. A temperature of 1000°C is needed to fuse sand and salt.

During the Bronze Age (3150–1050 BC), glass was a luxury material, found in palaces and exchanged as diplomatic gifts. The invention of glass-blowing in the middle of the first century BC made glass easier to produce, and it became accessible to many across the Roman Empire. Thanks to the unique properties of glass – it can be transparent, translucent or opaque, and it is odourless and tasteless – glass vessels became particularly attractive for serving food and drink. Broken vessels could simply be melted down for recycling.

Above: Flinders Petrie's handwritten notes for his unpublished manuscript 'Glass and Glazing'.

Left: A glass fish that would have been attached to a rare type of glass vessel from the Roman Empire. Third or fourth century AD. Purchased by Flinders Petrie (UC22418).

The Petrie Museum collection includes more than 2,000 Roman, Byzantine and Islamic glass objects from Egypt, ranging in date from the mid-first century BC to the early nineteenth century AD. There are vessels and bracelets, rings and beads, gaming pieces and glass weights. Over half of this collection comes from excavations at Oxyrhynchus in the Fayum – a site well known for the thousands of Greek papyri found in its rubbish dumps. No other museum has such a large collection of glass from a single ancient town.

Modern analysis of glass fragments from Oxyrhynchus uses an electron-microprobe, a method by which a small sample of an object is bombarded with an electron beam. This determines the exact chemical composition of the material. As the type of sand differs on each coastline, the chemical composition can tell us where the raw glass was produced. Preliminary results suggest that the people of Oxyrhynchus were using raw glass produced in Egypt, probably in furnaces in the Wadi Natrun and the northern coast of Sinai. There are very few examples of imported glass, for example from the Levant. What led to this preference for local products? Was it simply a question of cost? Or was the Egyptian glass just more beautiful?

Daniela Rosenow

Right: A 1,800-year-old glass flask excavated from a grave at Saft el-Henna in the Nile Delta (UC22057).

'She smites the legions of men': a Greek goddess in Egypt

Upon her head she placed the helmet with two horns and with four bosses, forged of gold ... Then she stepped upon the flaming chariot and grasped her spear, heavy and huge and strong, with which she smites the legions of men ...

This is how the Greek goddess Athena went to war. It is just one small snippet of an epic ancient myth that survives on a small, 1,700-year-old pottery sherd and several very fragmentary pieces of papyri in the Petrie collection. The full epic poem, *The Iliad*, was supposedly composed by Homer but was intended to be recited rather than read. It tells the story of the war against Troy and the siege of the city by different Greek states, who finally infiltrated the city in a wooden horse. In the poem, the gods and goddesses took sides in the war as well, protecting their favourites from harm or smiting their enemies. The conflict was started by the Trojan prince, Paris, who was made to choose the most beautiful goddess out of three: Athena, the goddess of wisdom and war; Hera, the goddess of marriage; and Aphrodite, the goddess of love. Unsurprisingly, he chose Aphrodite, who caused Helen, a married woman, to fall in love and run away to Troy with Paris. In the subsequent 10–year war, the losing goddesses backed the Greeks out of spite for Paris' slight.

The Greeks were fascinated with Egypt as a centre of knowledge, and even before the conquest of Egypt by Alexander the Great in 332 BC, there were colonies of Greek settlers living in cities in the Egyptian Delta such as Naukratis. According to Herodotus, the city of Sais was of great interest to Athenians, with the city's patron goddess, Neith, being identified as a manifestation of Athena.[34] Ancient authors, including Diodorus Siculus, proposed that the Greek Athenians were colonists from Egyptian Sais.[35] Prominent Athenians, on the other hand, such as Solon, visited the Egyptian city and postulated a connection between the destruction of the original colony in Greece and the god-wrought punishment of Atlantis that was levied due to its military aggression against both Egypt and Greece. Athena is the subject of statues and terracotta figurines and was depicted on lamps and coins in ancient Egypt. One such image was published by Petrie in his journal *Ancient Egypt*: a leaden token with a bust of Athena wearing her crested helmet (shown opposite). Petrie suggests in this 1913 publication that these tokens may be fake coins, but they may have also functioned as theatre tickets or even humble offerings to the goddess.

Edmund Connolly

Above: Sherd of pottery with parts of the Greek literary text *The Iliad* written on it (UC31894).

Left: Pottery fragment from Naukratis (540 BC) depicting a Greek soldier (UC19361).

Opposite: Ancient Greek silver coin with the head of Athena on one side and an owl, her symbol, on the other (UC39201).

Journeys to the Afterlife

For the ancient Egyptians the journey to the Afterlife was full of hazards. Having the aid of a set of spells of protection and guidance, called by Egyptologists the 'Book of the Dead', was therefore a good investment. Around 300–200 BC someone bought just such an insurance policy, written on linen bandages that were probably placed in an Egyptian tomb. It was intended to remain beside the deceased for eternity, but the 'book' had an afterlife of its own.

The textile fragment above shows one of the most crucial scenes in the 'Book of the Dead': the weighing of the heart. For the Egyptians, the heart, not the brain, was where memories, intelligence and emotions were stored, so by weighing the heart a person's life could be judged. If the heart was found to be heavier than the feather of truth (*Ma'at*) then it would be tossed into the gaping jaws of a demon, rendering the deceased incapable of entering the Afterlife.

We do not know who the owner of this 'Book of the Dead' fragment was or how the linen bandages left the owner's Egyptian tomb. After they were removed from the ancient burial place, though, the bandages were cut into pieces and the resulting fragments made their separate ways around the globe. One of the fragments was eventually acquired by William MacGregor (1848–1937), a British collector who formed an impressive collection of Egyptian antiquities in the late nineteenth and early twentieth centuries. The fragment was not in his possession for long and in 1922 it was on the move again. Sotheby's sale of the MacGregor Collection was a major event and almost a quarter of all the lots offered ended up being purchased by Henry Wellcome, the pharmaceutical

Above: Fragment of the 'Book of the Dead' found at Sedment and belonging to Khnumemheb (UC1295–1186 BC), showing the 'weighing of the heart' (UC32365).

magnate. Wellcome had poured large quantities of his vast wealth into buying things for his Medical Museum, most of which were never displayed. On his death millions of objects – 'an infinity of things'[36] – had piled up in several warehouses across London. Among the sea of artefacts were thousands of ancient Egyptian items that came to the Petrie Museum for dispersal in 1964, including the fragment that is now numbered UC32432. The ancient inscriptions on this fragment are now accompanied by many modern inscriptions that record these more recent journeys: MacGregor Collection numbers, Sotheby's sales lot numbers, Wellcome Collection numbers and finally its Petrie Museum accession number. In a sense then, while people collect objects, objects also collect people as they journey through the ages.

Alice Stevenson

U.C.16773.

Living images: funerary portraits from Roman times

She was 'a young married woman of about 25; of a sweet but dignified expression, with beautiful features, and of a fine complexion'.[37] Flinders Petrie was captivated. The lady in question had died almost 2,000 years earlier in the first or second century AD, but her image was still vivid and striking millennia later, captured in a painting on a thin wooden panel known as a 'mummy portrait'.

Petrie excavated a large number of mummy portraits from a cemetery near the pyramid of Hawara during two seasons of work, first in 1888–89 and again in 1910–11. They caused great excitement when they were shown in London at Petrie's annual summer exhibition, as they were seen – rightly or wrongly – as the first 'true portraits' in world history. The Petrie Museum today holds the largest collection of these Roman-period funerary panels outside of Egypt, with some fifty-three individuals represented. The other finds were split between the Cairo Museum and around thirty-six institutions worldwide.

What had allowed this woman's picture to survive the centuries was the use of a particular type of long-lasting paint called tempera, which had been mixed with a beeswax binding medium. The panels were then secured within the complex mummy wrappings of elite individuals of the Fayum region. The question of the use of these 'portraits' in life remains unanswered, but we know from Petrie's excavation records that the human remains to which they were attached seem to have been buried with very little care.

Above: Photograph of a portrait mummy from the 1911 excavations, lying half uncovered in a mud-brick chamber (PMAN 1263).

Below: Portrait of a man (UC19613).

After two millennia underground many of the mummies and portraits were too damaged or fragile to travel and Petrie was forced to invent methods of temporary conservation – with varying degrees of success. Petrie thought that the portraits 'should be treated eventually just like any other old pictures; carefully cleaned, and then varnished with the best copal varnish'.[38] A century later, it is clear that such interventions were not enough and renewed conservation became an increasing priority. After the re-opening of the present Petrie Museum following a major refit in 1988, the Museum's Curator, Barbara Adams, found conservators prepared to do the work, but there was no money for the huge task. Barbara came up with the idea of starting a Museum 'Friends' group as part of a fundraising appeal. Thus the Friends of the Petrie Museum was born. The conservation project took ten years to complete and forms one of the many contributions the Friends have made to the conservation, display and publication of the Museum collection.

After Barbara's death in 2002 the Friends of Petrie Museum supported the publication of a volume in her honour and a catalogue of the portraits seemed a fitting tribute.[39]

Jan Picton

U.C.14692.

'Tis the Season: annual exhibitions in archaeology

'… I found myself quite unexpectedly in the presence of the dead …'

So sayeth 'Jackdaw', a reviewer for the *Leeds Mercury* in June 1888. Entering Egyptian Hall on Piccadilly he saw Flinders Petrie's exhibition of antiquities from Hawara. Viewing mummies some two thousand years old in this intimate setting prompted him to 'uncover' – a Victorian euphemism meaning to remove his hat as a mark of respect. He was struck by the freshness of the objects on display.[40]

During Petrie's Hawara excavations in 1887–88, a series of Roman-era mummy cases had been discovered, featuring remarkably lifelike portraits of their dead inhabitants. At that point, two businessmen, Henry Martyn Kennard and Jesse Haworth, were financially supporting Petrie's excavations. On Petrie's behalf Kennard rented 'the large square room' in Egyptian Hall, a now demolished building with Egyptianesque architectural embellishments, to enable Petrie to showcase his work. Built in the early nineteenth century as a museum, Egyptian Hall became a popular entertainment venue and art gallery.

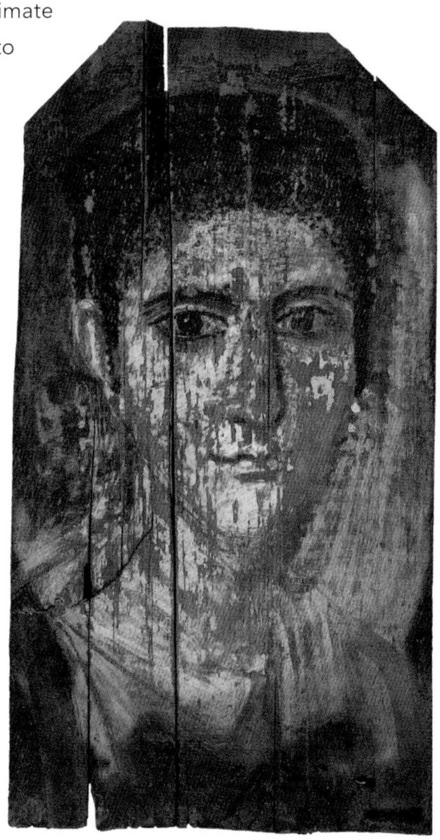

With no direct governmental support at this time, British archaeologists depended on public subscriptions and private patronage in order to continue excavating. After excavation came exhibition – mainly during the all-important London 'Season' when the well-to-do flooded the capital, bringing daughters and sons to the marriage market, and indulged in cultural and social delights of all varieties.[41] In 1888 the 'annual exhibition', a temporary display of excavated objects, plans and artwork from archaeological sites, was in its early stages. As the twentieth century dawned a cadre of British archaeologists, archaeological societies and expedition teams were using annual exhibitions across the capital to engage public interest and secure financing for continuing research.

The Hawara exhibition ran for four weeks, from 18 June to 12 July 1888, attracting an estimated 2,000 people.[42] It has been speculated that Oscar Wilde may have been among that number, perhaps drawing inspiration for his 1891 novel *The Picture of Dorian Gray* from the ancient portraits.[43] The exhibition's impact was still strong three months later; a *Chambers's Journal* review compared two portraits of young girls to the 'professional beauties of the present day'.[44] Perhaps one of them was UC38103, shown here – a faded yet evocative portrait of a young woman. Replace the tunic with a gown, and she could be a late Victorian lady of fashion, with her hair piled on the top of her head – a Roman-era Mary of Teck (from 1893 Princess of Wales). Along with all the other Hawara objects, she masks a hidden history of archaeological display in London.

Amara Thornton

Above: Portrait panel painting of a young woman excavated at Hawara (UC38103).

Opposite: Portrait panel painting of a young man excavated at Hawara in 1888 (UC19612).

Right: Photograph of
the temporary annual
exhibition in London,
1911, of archaeological
finds from Hawara.
Petrie Musuem Archives.

The archaeology of race: Petrie's Memphis heads

Among the numerous trays in the cupboards of the Petrie Museum is one marked 'Memphis "Race" Heads'. This drawer contains fifty-seven small heads, probably from terracotta figurines, that date from the Ptolemaic or Roman period. The occasional original typed label on yellowing paper lies beside them, with classifications such as 'Sumerian'. They are only a small fraction of about 300 heads preserved in the Petrie Museum collection, though no other drawer is similarly marked. It is clear from this tag just how profound Flinders Petrie's interest in race and racial types was. This collection of 'Race' heads was probably put together by Petrie for teaching purposes; his work on racial typologies influenced him so much that he believed students of Egyptian archaeology needed to understand the importance of establishing racial difference through looking at representations of the face.[45]

Petrie thought that these heads 'were the figures of more than a dozen races' made by Graeco-Egyptian artists, carefully recording 'foreigners' in the city of Memphis.[46] Sometimes he used contemporary examples from his own period to ascribe identities to these heads. He argued, for example, that one head (UC48515) was 'Hebrew' due to the facial 'resemblance to a modern Jewish Type coming from Germany'. Another head (UC8457), Petrie described as a Persian and commented that it shows the 'high-bred Aryan type', considering the Persian Empire as a 'magnificent creation' that established world peace from the Indus to the Balkans.

The production of terracotta heads and figurines took place across the Hellenistic world from 350 to 40 BC. It is extremely difficult to ascertain what their purpose was;

Left: Drawer from the Petrie Museum containing Petrie's series of 'Memphis "Race" Heads'.

they could have held votive, decorative or medical functions, or a mixture of the three. The heads found at Memphis belong to four different periods: Ptolemaic Egyptian, Hellenistic Greek, Romano-Egyptian and Roman. Sally-Ann Ashton has further categorized these heads into subject areas, such as Egyptian priests, divinities, rulers, caricatures, festival participants and actors.[47] We know from written evidence that Memphis was a diverse city comprising groups of Jewish, Greek, Macedonian Greek, Egyptian, Persian and other peoples. These terracotta heads may give a glimpse of ethnic and cultural diversity in Ptolemaic Memphis.

The heads might show the caricatures of the ancient world or the stereotypes of the modern world; much depends on the viewpoint of the person looking at them. Petrie's emphasis on racial types in reading these heads, and the lack of archaeological information about them, makes interpretation problematic. We have Petrie's vision of Greek artists recording 'racial types' in Ptolemaic Memphis, which is not unrelated to the more contemporary idea that the heads simply reflect urban ethnic diversity.

Debbie Challis

Hakubutsukan: Egypt between East Asia and England

There are many artefacts in the Petrie which seem to have absolutely nothing whatsoever to do with a museum of Egyptian archaeology. These include a Korean bronze mirror, engraved with a motif of a Chinese phoenix, gifted by a Japanese archaeologist. The story behind the mirror, however, reveals an important set of relationships between the development of archaeology in the West and in the East.

Between 1914 and 1917 a young Japanese archaeologist from the Kyoto Imperial University, Kosaku Hamada, visited Britain in order to learn more about European approaches to archaeology. Flinders Petrie was one of the Western scholars with whom he stayed during this time. On his return to Japan, Hamada was appointed as Kyoto University's first Professor of Archaeology, a position from which he advocated what became the main tradition of Japanese archaeology to the next generation of Japanese scholars. That tradition was heavily informed by Petrie's approach to archaeology, which emphasized rigorous typological classifications and systematic fieldwork.

Below: A Korean bronze mirror with motif of a Chinese phoenix, dating between the tenth and the fourteenth century AD (UC25494).

Right: Three copper implements from the tombs surrounding the funerary enclosure of the Dynasty 1 king Djet (UC16174–UC16176).

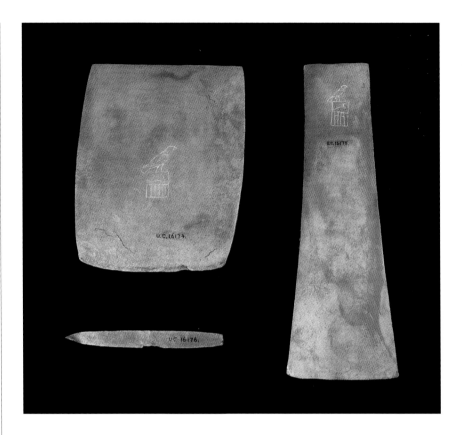

Hamada carried out extensive fieldwork in Japan and Korea and he maintained contact with Flinders Petrie. Many of Hamada's students followed in his footsteps, travelling to learn archaeology in London, and they translated abstracts of recent Japanese archaeological publications into English. These articles on Japanese archaeology were then, somewhat incongruously, included in the magazine *Ancient Egypt* that Petrie edited.

In 1922 Petrie allocated to the fledgling Kyoto University's Hakubutsukan (the Japanese word for 'museum'), a large concession of ancient Egyptian objects that collectively were 'typical of the style of each period'. In so doing, Petrie allowed his vision of Egyptian archaeology to be displayed in Japan. His division, however, split up assemblages recovered from the same tomb, resulting in associated objects being housed in museums on opposite sides of the globe. This included the contents of a 5,000-year-old grave found beside the funerary enclosures of one of the first rulers of Egypt at Abydos. Three copper implements from Tomb 387 bearing the name of king Djet remain in London in the Petrie Museum, but the pottery and the tomb owner's skull are today in Japan. It is one of many connections that link Egypt, East Asia and England.

Alice Stevenson

From China to Sudan

Set among the ancient Egyptian hieroglyphs, the Greek letters and the Arabic script, the Chinese characters spelling out *Qing Xiang* (meaning 'clear and fragrant') seem out of place. Yet these words, impressed onto a stoneware storage jar fragment, are also part of the history of Egypt and Sudan. The fragment is one of a dozen or so pieces of Chinese pottery from the thirteenth and fourteenth centuries AD found in Sudan and now held in the Petrie collection. Despite being so far removed from where they were made, in places such as the Guangdong and Fujian provinces of China, it is still possible to trace their histories. They offer a glimpse into trade relations between Africa, the Middle East and South East Asia some 700 years ago, and cast a spotlight onto imperial politics and collecting in the early twentieth century.

The porcelain and stoneware pieces were found at the Sudanese Red Sea port of Aidhab ('Aydhab). From around the tenth to the twelfth centuries AD Aidhab was an important and bustling harbour for pilgrims travelling to Mecca, traders selling cotton and glass from Egypt and Sudan, and merchants carrying cargos of spices and Chinese porcelain from Asia.[48] It was a different sort of traveller, however, who picked up these fragments in 1930: the colonial administrator for the British Empire in Sudan, Sir Douglas Newbold (1894–1945), who became Governor of Kordafan in 1933. Newbold had also been a regular contributor on archaeology in the journal *Sudan Notes and Records*,[49] in which passing reference was made to the fragments.[50]

Personal and colonial connections led these fragments to the Petrie Museum, as they passed from Newbold to his sister Kathleen Terry, and then to one of Newbold's friends: the Petrie Museum's Curator Anthony John Arkell (1898–1980), who cared for the collection from 1948 to 1963. Arkell had himself served in the Sudan Political Service after the First World War and was the first commissioner for Archaeology and Anthropology in Sudan in 1939, organizing the museums and ethnography collections at Khartoum as well as editing the journal *Sudan Notes and Records*.

Sudan Notes and Records was established by the colonial administration to, in part, foster Sudanese nationalism through archaeological research. This was part of the broader aim of British Indirect Rule Policy in the 1920s to shift Sudan away from revolutionary Egyptian ambitions, by developing Sudanese identity against Egyptian claims of sovereignty.[51] Despite the small size of these fragments, then, condensed around them are much wider geographies and histories that stretch across the centuries and the continents.

Debbie Challis

Opposite: Examples of Chinese sherds in the Petrie Museum found in Sudan (UC25796).

Below: Douglas Newbold's calling card.

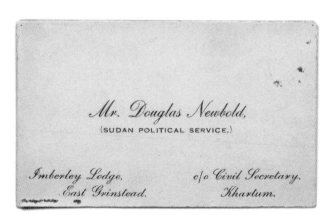

The ancient Kushite city of Meroe

Many visitors to the Petrie Museum will probably assume that most objects on display are Egyptian. In fact, many objects in the collection are from Sudan. The achievements of the ancient Egyptians are well known to most people, but those of their neighbours in Sudan much less so. Relatively few people know that Sudan was once home to great ancient civilizations.[52]

One such Sudanese object is a faience *ankh* inscribed with the name of the king Aspelta (opposite). It was perhaps held during religious ceremonies or used as a votive offering. The *ankh* is based on the Egyptian hieroglyph for 'life' and was probably intended to ensure the king's longevity.

The Second Kingdom of Kush was based in Sudan. For almost a thousand years, from the time of the ancient Greeks to the end of the western Roman Empire in the fifth century AD, this now almost forgotten Nile Valley empire flourished. It was one of the ancient world's most stable civilizations, which for a period as the Dynasty 25 ruled over Egypt as well as Sudan.

Aspelta ruled this kingdom from 593 to 568 BC. Although he was buried at Nuri, the *ankh* was found in the remains of Meroe city. Meroe was to become the final urban capital of the politically stable Kushite kingdom. It was the last of the great ancient cities in Sudan's long and impressive history. The Greek historian, Herodotus, for example wrote that Meroe was a great city and was said to be the capital of Ethiopia.[53]

Archaeologists have divided Meroe into three main districts: the Royal City, the Temple of Amun and the structures around it, and the town itself.[54] The Royal City contained temples, palatial dwellings and a water sanctuary. The water sanctuary's decorations included inlaid faience discs and panels.

The remains of the Second Kingdom of Kush are evident, though often overlooked. The *ankh* inscribed for Aspelta is one of thousands of artefacts from this ancient society which are in museums today. Near the remains of Meroe city are the ruins of eighty-four pyramids where generations of Kushite kings, queens and elite people are buried. Papyri and inscriptions in the Meroitic script have survived, but despite the many written sources, no-one has yet been able to translate the language. Understanding the Kingdom of Kush aids our understanding of the whole ancient Nile Valley.

The faience *ankh* inscribed for Aspelta signified the desire of the Kushites for their king's endurance and revival during his lifetime. It has survived thousands of years. This *ankh*, and the civilization it represents, are ready for our renewed attention.

Kandace Chimbiri

Above: Fragment of stone with text written in the Meroitic language (UC44174).

Opposite: Faience *ankh*, the Egyptian symbol for life, inscribed with the name of King Aspelta (UC43949).

He Tells Tales of Meroe

As if his croak sounds from stone itself
As if his voice in darkness is stained with the timbre of eternity

When I first saw him alone, lost in thought,
poised behind glass,
I recalled how his sperm had once spawned from the suck of motherly mud
to snatch prey with spit
A camouflaged trickster,
awakening each spring with his mates
to a spring of mating

Now an enigmatic relic behind glass,
perhaps he tells tales of Meroe –
witness to that city's sad trajectory from glory to dejection

In this, his last siesta,
he readies himself for life
with his new cloak, a new tongue and his crown [55]

Al-Saddiq Al-Raddi
Translated from the Arabic by Sarah Maquire and Rashid Elsheikh

This poem was written during Al-Saddiq Al-Raddi's residency at the Petrie Museum, thanks to a partnership with the Poetry Translation Centre and funding from Arts Council England. He worked with objects from the Sudanese royal city of Meroe, the residence of Kushite royalty from the sixth century BC, and a site that has more standing pyramids than in Egypt. 'He Tells Tales of Meroe' was read in Arabic by Saddiq to a packed Museum of poetry-lovers in May 2014, bringing new life to the Museum's objects.

Left: Saddiq in the Petrie Museum, examining an object from the Meroe royal bath house.
© Crispin Hughes.

Opposite: The Meroitic limestone frog that inspired Al-Saddiq Al-Raddi's poem 'He Tells Tales of Meroe' (UC43984).

'Camel, O camel, come and fetch and carry': on two camels

The image of camels striding between the pyramids, against the backdrop of the desert dunes and the blazing sun, is a romantic one. Yet camels were only introduced to Egypt on a large scale under the Persians (from 525 BC), although they are sporadically attested in Egypt before this. From the Ptolemaic period (323–30 BC), they became the main transport animal for the desert. Camels – in Egypt the evidence is mostly for one-humped dromedaries, although two-humped Bactrian camels were also used – occur in their greatest numbers in the written and textual evidence of the first to eighth centuries AD, long after the last pharaohs.

Two completely preserved terracottas in the Petrie Museum, UC48026 (below) and UC48033, show the camel as a beast of burden and means of transportation. The first camel has a saddle and amphorae rack, on each side of which are three amphorae. Hanging from the front of the rack, down the forelegs, are plant bundles, possibly flowers, while the neckband of the harness has pendent ornaments. The second camel, with a saddle and painted reins, is slightly bigger.

Both figures are hollow and made in two halves from moulds (such as UC33303). Traces of red paint on the neck of the first survives, while white paint covers the surface of the second, with areas of red and black paint that highlight different features. These traces hint at the original appearance of the figures, which were cheaply produced and brightly painted to make up for their basic form.

Little is known about their discovery, although both figures are recorded as being from the city of Memphis and they are dated respectively to the Roman (first or second century) and Byzantine (fifth or sixth century) periods. That they were mass-produced is evident by the presence of a terracotta camel in the British Museum (EA 37628) that comes from the same mould as the figurine below. The British Museum's camel is said to come from the Fayum, which is where such objects were first found in large numbers.

What they were used for is also unclear. One has a suspension hole through the base of its neck, showing that it was hung, although where and on what is unknown. Terracotta figures have been found in both tombs and domestic buildings. They may have been used as toys, votive offerings, or as sources of protection and good luck.

By the end of the third century AD, camels came to be associated with the Coptic saint, Menas. According to legend, after his death the camel bearing his body lay down in the desert south of Alexandria and refused to move. Menas was buried at that spot. In the fourth century 'the house of Mena' (Karm Abu Mena) was built for the thousands of pilgrims who flocked to the site. Many would have received a ceramic pilgrim flask (*ampulla*), like the one opposite, with a depiction of St Menas standing between two camels, which could be used to take water from a healing spring associated with him near Alexandria.

Above: Photograph from Margaret Murray's album, showing camels near Petrie's excavations at Abydos, around 1902. Petrie Museum archives.

Below: Mould-made terracotta camel figurine (UC48026).

Opposite: Pottery pilgrim flask stamped with an image of the Christian martyr St Menas (UC19516).

Jennifer Cromwell

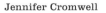

Composed of air and light: a rare survival from medieval Egypt

With its sad-looking broken legs, tail and ears, this animal-shaped container seen opposite may look unprepossessing, but it is in fact one of only around 200 rock crystal objects that survive from medieval Egypt. Petrie is thought to have bought this small rock crystal animal in Memphis on 1 March 1908.

Rock crystal, a form of quartz, was particularly highly prized during the rule of the Fatimid dynasty (AD 969–1171). Ahmad al-Maqrizi (d. AD 1442) wrote a *History of the Fatimids* and tells us that the treasury of the Caliphs included more than 17,000 crystal objects. Al-Maqrizi's source was probably court official Ibn al-Zubayr's 'Book of Gifts and Rarities', which cites 36,000 examples of cut glass and rock crystal. This popularity is partly due to the fact that rock crystal was believed to have magical or prophylactic properties – drinking from a crystal vessel could, for example, cure nightmares or permanently ward off thirst. Postulated by some medieval Islamic scholars to be composed of air and light, rock crystal was connected with the religious beliefs of the Fatimids. In the *Qur'an* (XXXVII, *sura al-saffat*, vv. 45–7) it is associated with life in Paradise.

Rock crystal also appealed because it was rare and completely transparent. The raw crystal was imported from various regions, but also found in Egypt in the Western Desert and Sinai. It was difficult to work (which might explain the rather elongated form of the creature in the Petrie), and only a few centres of production are known. Persian traveller Nasir Khusraw (d. AD 1088) describes a visit to the Suq al Qanadil (Lamp Market) in Cairo, where he saw rock crystal being carved.

So why have so few rock crystal vessels from this period survived? Social disturbances and the bankruptcy of the Fatimid state in the eleventh century led to the pillaging of the court treasury and a dispersal of its famed treasures, including the thousands of rock crystal objects. Some came to Europe in the Middle Ages, often as reliquaries, and can now be found in the treasuries of churches.

The Petrie crystal container has a hole drilled under the chin of the animal and into its body. Several museum collections include small zoomorphic containers, but scholars cannot agree on their purpose. They would not be very efficient as perfume or unguent containers since the horizontal shape might lead to spillage. Some may have contained amulets, a good fit with the prophylactic and magical aspects of the crystal.

But what is the animal now in the Petrie? The most popular creature in Fatimid art is the hare, and in particular the running hare, which is often seen with or surrounded by grapevines. It represented good fortune, and fertility in the sense of the sustainment of life. It is difficult to be absolutely sure because of the broken ears and legs, but a stylized hare is the most likely identification of the Petrie piece, legs up as he runs along, and ears flying behind him in the wind: a small but very significant reminder of the vibrant luxury of medieval Egypt.

Carolyn Perry

Opposite: Rock crystal container in the shape of a hare (UC25300).

'To my wife, on whose toil most of my work has depended': women on excavation

On 10 March 1923, the *London Illustrated News* ran a double-page spread with the headline 'Men who perform the "spade work" of history: British names famous in the field of archaeology'. Many familiar faces from Egyptology were featured, including Flinders Petrie, Howard Carter, and F. L. Griffith. What this feature completely overlooked, as many histories of 'Great Discoveries' have, is the important contribution made by female archaeologists. Indeed, many excavations in Egypt and Sudan were dependent upon them.

Women were frequently members of fieldwork campaigns in Egypt and they shared with the whole team the discomforts of life in the field: the dirt, the discoveries and the physical labour. Petrie's wife, Hilda, was one such 'trowelblazer'. She set out for Egypt for her first excavation in 1896, only a few hours after marrying Flinders Petrie. For her, fieldwork represented 'a splendid free open life ... without the ordinary necessities in so many ways'.[56]

During field seasons Hilda Petrie engaged in one of the most important activities on excavation: the recording of finds and the inking onto objects of the record of their findspot. Many objects in the Petrie Museum bear her handwriting and these form indispensable keys that allow us to associate those things with the records, plans and photographs that document the circumstances of their discovery. Throughout her career Hilda additionally undertook the surveying and planning of sites, inked drawings for publication and edited her husband's text. Hilda was also instrumental in raising funds for expeditions. For these reasons, Petrie dedicated his final memoirs of a life in archaeology 'to my wife, on whose toil most of my work has depended'.[57]

Many other female pioneers in archaeology also acquired their first experiences of fieldwork on Petrie digs. This included Gertrude Caton-Thompson, who not only made ground-breaking discoveries in Egyptian prehistory, but additionally went on to demonstrate definitively the indigenous African origins of Great Zimbabwe in the face of hostile criticism from the largely male academy. Other regular field collaborators included artists such as Winifred Brunton and Annie Quibell, whose toil on site is often little recognized, but was crucial to the success of field seasons.

Alice Stevenson

Above: Predynastic palette from Hu, numbered by Hilda Petrie on site (UC10886).

Opposite: Hilda Petrie descending a tomb-shaft by rope-ladder, perhaps at Denderah 1897–98. Petrie Museum archive (PMAN3176).

Right: Sunrise at the excavation camp at Oxyrhynchus, painted by Flinders Petrie (Petrie Museum archives).

'The largest and the only fully dated collection': Xia Nai and Egyptian beads

It was one of the areas of the new Museum in 1915 that Flinders Petrie was most proud of. He would often boast in publications that it was the biggest, most representative collection to be found anywhere in the world.[58] He was speaking not about pottery, but about beads, of which there are some 3,000 strings in the collection.

These ornaments were created with almost every material, colour and texture imaginable and they come from across Egypt and beyond: vibrant blue lapis lazuli from Afghanistan, glossy black obsidian from Turkey, and aqua-green turquoise from the Sinai. A single etched carnelian bead also demonstrates that artefacts from India's Indus Valley found their way to Egypt in the late Middle Kingdom (UC30334). Gold, electrum and silver are all represented in the collection, as well as pierced shells, animal teeth and fossils. There are even beads made of meteorites (see Out of this world, p.30). Such adornments were worn by men, women and children in a multitude of ways: as necklaces, bracelets, girdles, anklets, diadems and hair braids. There is a fossil shark's tooth that once belonged to a Neolithic pastoralist (UC2909), a string of beads retrieved from the dust of a sarcophagus in a royal tomb (UC6766), and a poignant set of pendants that had been placed in a modest infant's coffin under the floor of an ancient home (UC18628).

Despite the richness of beads as evidence for ancient social identities, craftwork and trade, the study of such a huge corpus of material is a daunting task. Even some of Petrie's most thorough students, who were committed to full artefact documentation, confessed that dealing with beads was 'infinitely more tiresome' than the description of any other type of artefact.[59] The seemingly indefatigable Petrie himself, who had every good intention of synthesizing the mass of material into a corpus just as he had with so many other object categories, was defeated by the enormity of the undertaking.

The mammoth effort to systematize the thousands of individual components was eventually taken on by a cheerful young Chinese scholar who examined the entire series for his PhD thesis. That young scholar was Xia Nai, a man who became one of China's leading archaeologists and pioneers after the founding of the People's Republic in 1949. Xia Nai wrote works on coins, jade, silks and astronomy, but his account of the Petrie bead collection was not published until 2014.[60] Xia Nai's corpus of 1,760 index cards has also recently been placed online and his meticulous attention to detail is clear, exposing the diversity of materials, forms and periods represented in the collection. Ordered, classified and documented, they await a new generation of scholars' study and wider appreciation.

Alice Stevenson

Above: Examples of Xia Nai's card index, now held in the Petrie Museum archives.

Opposite: Gold cowrie shell beads from tomb 7923 at Qau, c. 2180–2025 BC (UC18092).

Below: Beads and amulets from Naqada South Town dating to 1295–1186 BC (UC29133)'

Right: Bead necklace excavated in 1891 at Amarna. Conservation revealed a turquoise bead inscribed with the name of Tutankhamun (UC1957).

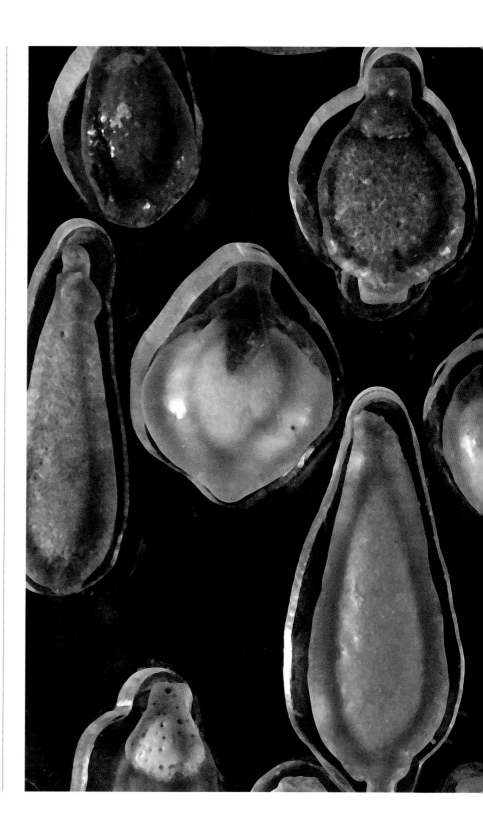

Notes

Introduction: a modest little museum

1 Letter from Petrie to Spurrell, 7 July 1879. A copy of the letter is in the Petrie Museum, but the original is held in Norwich Castle Museum.

2 Winslow, C. (1892) The Queen of Egyptology. *The American Antiquarian Reprint* compilation issue: pp. 1–15.

3 Biographical Notes, Amelia Edwards to Countess Ballestran, 8 January 1881, Amelia Edwards Papers, Somerville College Library, Oxford.

4 Edwards, A. (1891) My Home Life. *Arena* 4, pp. 541–43.

5 Petrie, W. M. F. (1915) The Egyptian Museum, University College. *Egyptian Archaeology* 2(4), p.169.

6 E.g. Murray, M. (1921) *The Witch-Cult in Western Europe*. Oxford: Oxford University Press.

7 Cited in Drower, M. (1985) *Flinders Petrie. A Life in Archaeology*. London: Victor Gollancz, p. 320.

8 *The Times*, 5 March 1980.

9 Quirke, S. (2010) *Hidden Hands. Egyptian Workforces in Petrie Excavations*. London: Duckworth.

Out of this world: prehistoric space beads

10 Rehren, T. et al. (2013) 5,000 Years Old Egyptian Iron Beads Made from Hammered Meteoritic Iron. *Journal of Archaeological Science* 40, pp. 4785–92.

Abu Bagousheh: Father of Pots

11 Petrie, W. M. F and Quibell, J. (1896) *Naqada and Ballas*. London: Bernard Quaritch, p. 8.

Lost and found: the rediscovery of the Tarkhan dress

12 Hall, R. (2001) *Egyptian Textiles*. Shire Egyptology: Aylesbury.

13 Landi, S. and Hall, R. M. (1979) The Discovery and Conservation of an Ancient Egyptian Linen Tunic. *Studies in Conservation* 24, pp. 141–52.

The lost lions of Koptos

14 Adams, B. (1984) *The Koptos Lions*. Milwaukee: Milwaukee Public Museum.

A face in the crowd: chance encounters with Egyptian sculpture

15 Petrie, W. M. F. (1915) The Egyptian Museum, University College. *Egyptian Archaeology* 2(4), p. 168.

16 Ibid.

17 Walmsley, A. (1992) *The Caribbean Artists Movement 1966–1972: A Literary & Cultural History*. London and Port of Spain : New Beacon Books, p. 31.

Ali Suefi of Lahun and the gold cylinder

18 Engelbach, R. (1923) *Harageh*. London: British School of Archaeology in Egypt, p. 16.

Seth: seductions and stelae

19 Petrie, W. M. F. (1890) *Kahun, Gurob and Hawara*. London: Kegan Paul.

20 Griffith F. Ll. (1898) *The Petrie Papyri: Hieratic Papyri from Kahun and Gurob (Principally of the Middle Kingdom)*. London: Bernard Quaritch.

21 Parkinson, R. B. (1995) 'Homosexual' Desire and Middle Kingdom Literature. *The Journal of Egyptian Archaeology* 81, pp. 57–76.

Termites and tapioca: the survival of Amarna's colours

22 Petrie, W. M. F. (1931) *Seventy Years in Archaeology*. London: Marston & Co., p. 139.

23 Drower, M. (2004) *Letters from the Desert. The Correspondence of Flinders and Hilda Petrie*. Oxford: Aris & Phillips, p. 82.

24 Petrie, W. M. F. (1894) *Tell el Amarna*. London: Aris & Phillips, p. 2.

25 Drower, M. (1985) *Flinders Petrie. A Life in Archaeology*. London: Aris & Phillips, p. 197.

'While skulls bobbed around on the waves …': retrieving Horwedja's *shabtis*

26 Petrie, W. M. F. (1931) *Seventy Years in Archaeology*. London: Marston & Co., p. 96.

27 Petrie, W. M. F. (1890) *Kahun, Gurob and Hawara*. London: Kegan Paul, p. 9.

28 Petrie Journal, Griffith Institute, University of Oxford, 13–19 January 1889.

29 Janes, G. (2012) *The Shabti Collections. A Selection from the Manchester Museum*. Lymm: Olicar House Publications: pp. 393–434.

30 UC28060, UC28061, UC28053, UC28054, UC28055, UC28667.

Miw: the Langton Cat Collection

31 Murray, M. (1940) Review of *The Cat in Ancient Egypt* by N. and B. Langton. *Bulletin of the School of Oriental and African Studies* 10, pp. 806–07.

32 See Malek, J. (1993) *The Cat in Ancient Egypt*. London: British Museum Press.

33 Langton, N. (1936) Notes on Some Small Egyptian Figurines of Cats. *The Journal of Egyptian Archaeology* 22(2), pp. 115–20.

'She smites the legions of men': a Greek goddess in Egypt

34 Herodotus, *The Histories*, 2.59; Plato, *Timaeus* 21e–25d; Plato, *Critias*.

35 Diodorus Siculus, *Library of History*, 1.28–29.

Journeys to the Afterlife

36 Larson, F. (2009) *An Infinity of Things: How Sir Henry Wellcome Collected the World*. Oxford: Oxford University Press.

Living images: funerary portraits from Roman times

37 Petrie's Journal, Griffith Institute, University of Oxford. 29 January–5 February 1888.

38 Ibid.

39 Picton, J., Quirke, S. and Roberts, P. (eds) (2007) *Living Images: Egyptian Funerary Portraits in the Petrie Museum*. New York: Left Coast Press.

'Tis the Season: annual exhibitions in archaeology

40 'Jackdaw' (1888) A Jackdaw's Flight. *Leeds Mercury*. 30 June.

41 Thornton, A. (2015) Exhibition Season: Annual Exhibitions in London, 1880s–1930s. *Bulletin of the History of Archaeology* 25(1):2, DOI: http://dx.doi.org/10.5334/bha.252.

42 Challis, D. (2013) *The Archaeology of Race: The Eugenic Ideas of Francis Galton and Flinders Petrie*. London: Bloomsbury Academic, p. 113.

43 Montserrat, D. (1997) Unidentified Human Remains: Mummies and the Erotics of Biography. In D. Montserrat (ed.) *Changing Bodies, Changing Meanings: Studies on the Human Body in Antiquity*. London and New York: Routledge, pp. 178–79.

44 Chambers, R. (ed.) (1888) Recent Discoveries in Egypt. *Chambers's Journal of Popular Literature, Science and Arts* 5 (249), 6 October, 640.

The archaeology of race: Petrie's Memphis heads

45 Challis, D. (2013) *The Archaeology of Race: The Eugenic Ideas of Francis Galton and Flinders Petrie*. London: Bloomsbury.

46 Petrie, W. M. F. (1909) *The Palace of Apries (Memphis II)*. London: British School of Archaeology in Egypt, p. 16.

47 Ashton, S-A. (2003) *Petrie's Ptolemaic and Roman Memphis*. London: Institute of Archaeology.

From China to Sudan

48 Insoll, T. (2003) *The Archaeology of Islam in Sub-Saharan Africa*. Cambridge: Cambridge University Press, pp. 93–97.

49 Collins, R. O. (n.d.) 'Newbold, Sir Douglas (1894–1945)', Oxford Dictionary of National Biography, Oxford University Press, 2004 [http://www.oxforddnb.com/view/article/35211, accessed 11 Nov 2014].

50 Hebbert, H. E. (1935) El Rih – A Red Sea Island. *Sudan Notes and Records* 18(2), p. 309.

51 Hamad, B. (1995) Sudan Notes and Records and Sudanese Nationalism, 1918–1956. *History in Africa* 22, pp. 239–70.

The ancient Kushite city of Meroe

52 For more, see K. N. Chimbiri (2011) *The Story of Early Ancient Egypt: Prehistoric and Old Kingdom Egypt (20,000–2181 B.C.)*. London: Golden Destiny.

53 Herodotus, *The Histories*, 2.29.

54 For more on this see Welsby, D. A. (2002) *The Kingdom of Kush*. London: British Museum Press.

He Tells Tales of Meroe

55 Original poem in Arabic © Al-Saddiq Al-Raddi 2015. English translation © Sarah Maguire and Rashid Elsheikh 2015.

'To my wife, on whose toil most of my work has depended': women on excavation

56 Drower, M. (1985) *Flinders Petrie: A Life in Archaeology*. London: Victor Gollancz.

57 Petrie, W. M. F. (1931) *Seventy Years in Archaeology*. London: Marston & Co.

'The largest and the only fully dated collection': Xia Nai and Egyptian beads

58 Petrie, W. M. F. (1915) The Egyptian Museum, University College. *Ancient Egypt* 2(4), pp. 168–80.

59 Mond, R. and Myres, O. H. (1937) *Armant*. London: Egypt Exploration Society, p.70.

60 Xia Nai (2014) *Ancient Egyptian Beads*. New York: Springer.

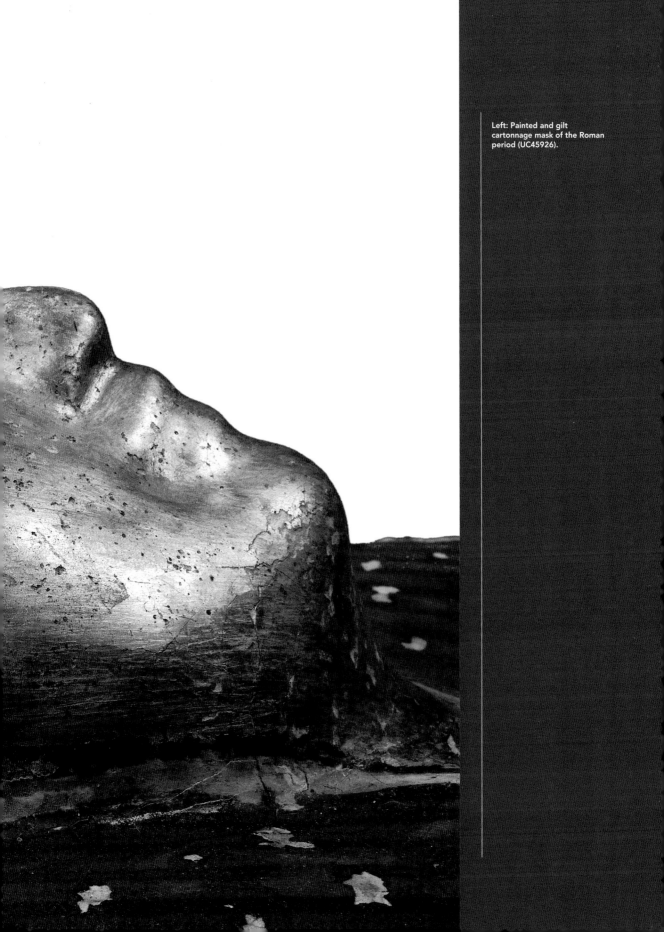

Further reading

Petrie Museum Collection:

Montserrat, D. 2000. *Digging for Dreams. Treasures from the Petrie Museum of Egyptian Archaeology University College London*. Glasgow: Glasgow City Council.

Picton, J. and Pridden, I. (eds) 2008. *Unseen Images. Archive Photographs in the Petrie Museum*. London: Golden House Publications.

Picton, J., Quirke, S., and Roberts, P. (eds) 2007. *Living Images. Egyptian Funerary Portraits in the Petrie Museum*. New York: Left Coast Press.

Quirke, S. 2010. *Hidden Hands. Egyptian Workforces in Petrie Excavation Archives, 1880–1924*. London: Duckworth.

Trope, B. T., Quirke, S. and Lacovara, P. (eds) 2005. *Excavating Egypt. Great Discoveries from the Petrie Museum of Egyptian Archaeology*. Atlanta: Michael C. Carlos Museum.

Petrie Museum Online:

Online catalogue: http://petriecat.museums.ucl.ac.uk

Digital Egypt: http://www.ucl.ac.uk/museums-static/digitalegypt//Welcome.html

3D Petrie: http://www.ucl.ac.uk/3dpetriemuseum

Histories of Flinders Petrie and Colleagues:

Carruthers, W. (ed.) 2014. *Histories of Egyptology. Disciplinary Measures*. London & New York: Routledge.

Challis, D. 2013. *The Archaeology of Race. The Eugenic Ideas of Francis Galton and Flinders Petrie*. London: Bloomsbury.

Colla, E. 2007. *Conflicted Antiquities. Egyptology, Egyptomania, Egyptian Modernity*. Durham, NC: Duke University Press.

Drower, M. 1985. *Flinders Petrie. A Life in Archaeology*. London: Victor Gollancz.

Drower, M. 2004. *Letters from the Desert. The Correspondence of Flinders and Hilda Petrie*. Oxford: Aris and Phillips.

Janssen, R. 1992. *The First Hundred Years. Egyptology at University College London 1892–1992*. London: UCL Press.

Moon, B. 2006. *More Usefully Employed. Amelia B. Edwards, Writer, Traveller and Campaigner for Ancient Egypt*. London: Egypt Exploration Society.

General Egyptian Archaeology

Bard, K. 2015. *An Introduction to the Archaeology of Ancient Egypt*. Second ed. Oxford: Wiley-Blackwell.

Timeline of Egyptian history

Date	Period	Subdivisions
400,000–8000 BC	Palaeolithic	Lower/Middle/Upper
8000–4000 BC	Neolithic	
4500–3800 BC	Badarian	
3800–3100 BC	Predynastic	Naqada I–III
3100–2686 BC	Early Dynastic	Dynasties 1–3
2686–2181 BC	Old Kingdom	Dynasties 4–6
2181–2025 BC	First Intermediate period	Dynasties 7–10
2025–1700 BC	Middle Kingdom	Dynasties 11–12
1700–1550 BC	Second Intermediate period	Dynasties 13–17
1550–1069 BC	New Kingdom	Dynasties 18–20
1069–664 BC	Third Intermediate period	Dynasties 21–25
664–332 BC	Late period	Dynasty 26
332–30 BC	Ptolemaic period	
30 BC – AD 395	Roman period	
395–641	Byzantine period	
641–1517	Islamic period	
1517–1805	Ottoman period	
1805–1919	Khedival period	
1919–1953	Monarchy	
1953–today	Republic	

Glossary

Ankh The hieroglyphic symbol for life.

Assemblage A group of artefacts found in association with each other.

Amarna period A particular time when the Egyptian capital was based near the modern village of Amarna. It was founded by King Akhenaten who made radical changes in religion and art, focused on the worship of the sun-god, the Aten.

Aten The depiction of the sun-god during the Amarna period in the form of the sun-disk.

Book of the Dead The modern name for a group of ancient Egyptian funerary spells and incantations that were intended to guide the dead through the underworld to the afterlife. The ancient Egyptians called these 'chapters for coming forth by day'.

Cartouche In ancient Egyptian hieroglyphic writing, an oval-shaped frame that contains a royal name.

Coptic The Egyptian language written with Greek letters, and some additional signs. It is strongly connected with Christianity in Egypt and was primarily used by Christians in the Byzantine and Islamic periods.

CT scan A computerized tomography (CT) *scan* that uses X-rays and a computer to create detailed images of the inside of the body.

Faience A glazed, non-clay ceramic material. It is composed mainly of crushed quartz or sand, with small amounts of lime and either natron or plant ash.

Hieratic A simplified form of ancient Egyptian writing used mainly for sacred purposes (hieratic means 'priestly').

Lower Egypt The northern region of Egypt that stretched from just south of modern-day Cairo to the Mediterranean Sea.

Mastaba An Arabic term meaning 'bench' that has been applied to the bench-shaped superstructure of certain types of Egyptian tomb.

Natron A naturally occurring salt mixture used in mummification to dry the body.

Nubia A region in today's southern Egypt and northern Sudan.

Scribe Ancient Egyptian official who could read and write.

Serekh A rectangular symbol representing the royal palace, in which one of the king's names was written.

Seriation A method of relative dating whereby artefacts and assemblages are sorted into a sequence, often with the aim of constructing a chronology.

Shabti (**or** *ushabti*) A funerary figurine placed in tombs from the Middle Kingdom onwards that took on corvee labour on behalf of the tomb owner in the Afterlife.

Sherd A broken piece of something brittle, usually used with reference to pottery.

Stela A stone, or occasionally wood, slab with an inscription on one side. In Egypt they are often found in the walls of chapels.

Stoneware A type of hard ceramic material.

Tempera A painting technique using water and egg mix as a binder.

Typology A system of classification used to group things on the basis of similarity and difference.

Upper Egypt The southern area of Egypt, from just south of Cairo to Aswan.

Opposite: Late Period pottery vessel with the face of the popular protector god Bes (UC8902).

Index

Friends of the Petrie Museum of Egyptian Archaeology

The Friends of the Petrie Museum were delighted to be invited to part-sponsor this centenary souvenir volume celebrating the Petrie Museum's wonderful collection.

The official Friends can only claim to have been supporting the Museum since 1988, but there is no doubt that it was the Museum's many friends – curators, lecturers, students, conservators, and passionate members of the public – who enabled the collection's survival through the tribulations of its first one hundred years, and you have met some of them in this volume.

The role of the Friends of the Petrie Museum is to fund conservation, display, publication and promotion of this world-class collection of Egyptian objects, so it seems fitting that our logo is the winged Isis – whose role as nurturer and protector we can only hope to emulate.

Above: Fragment of painted cartonnage, c. 915–715 BC (UC29805).

Why not join us?

In return for a modest annual subscription, our Friends enjoy a varied programme of events and a range of other benefits. More importantly, wherever you are in the world, if you join the Friends you are supporting this extraordinary Museum.

To find out more and to become a Friend of the Petrie Museum follow the link on the Museum webpage www.friendsofpetrie.org.uk/

Here's to the next one hundred years!